EXPLOR
INTERPRETI
BIBLICAL THEOLO   E PASTOR

EXPLORATIONS 11
INTERPRETING GOD'S PLAN: BIBLICAL THEOLOGY AND THE PASTOR

General Editor
R J Gibson

paternoster press

OPENBOOK
PUBLISHERS

First published in the UK 1998 by Paternoster Press

04 03 02 01 00 99 98   7 6 5 4 3 2 1

Paternoster Press is an imprint of Paternoster Publishing,
P.O. Box 300, Carlisle, Cumbria, CA3 0QS, U.K.
http://www.paternoster-publishing.com

British Library Cataloguing in Publication Data
A catalogue record for this book is available from the British Library.

ISBN 0-85364-881-6

Cover design by Mainstream, Lancaster
Typeset by WestKey Ltd, Falmouth, Cornwall
Printed in Great Britain by Mackays of Chatham plc

Contents

Preface

Since the early 1960s Moore College has included a subject called
Biblical Theology on its curriculum. This is unusual enough to
inspire both strong opinions and adverse comment, especially
since the eclipse of the so-called 'biblical theology movement' of
the mid-century. For our part, we are convinced that the subject
is a vital element of the theological course, and that the lack of it
constitutes an ongoing problem in many seminaries.

The 1996 School of Theology at Moore was devoted to this
issue. Three of the chief teachers in the subject over the years
since its inception were asked to contribute. They were Bishop
D. W. B. Robinson (who originally initiated the course), Dr
Graeme Goldsworthy (who has written two important books on
the subject) and Dr Barry Webb. Rev Michael Hill and I were
asked to address ethical and doctrinal issues respectively.

Moore College aims to produce preachers of God's word, the
Bible. When the pastor preaches to the congregation, or the
teacher addresses the class, he or she must be able to call on the
resources of a good theological education. The resources will
only be available in an atomistic form if there is no commitment
to the unity of Scripture. The exercise of biblical theology presupposes the inspiration of the Bible and demonstrates its unity.
It is fundamental to sound hermeneutical method. When biblical
theology is allied to doctrine, we have a pathway into Scripture
which enables us to read and explain it with confidence.

It is our hope that these papers will encourage others to
explore the riches of biblical theology and to incorporate it fully

into their approach to Scripture. Unless we can say to the church and the world what the bible says, Christian faith becomes mystical and superstitious and the clear statement of the gospel is lost.

Peter F. Jensen
Principal
Moore Theological College
May, 1997

Abbreviations Used In This Book

BBR	Bulletin for Biblical Research
EVQ	Evangelical Quarterly
IDB	Interpreter's Dictionary of the Bible
IVP	Inter-Varsity Press
LXX	The Septuagint (ancient Greek version of the Old Testament)
NT	New Testament
OT	Old Testament
RSV	The Revised Standard Version of the Bible
SCM	Student Christian Movement
SJT	Scottish Journal of Theology
SPCK	Society for the Promotion of Christian Knowledge
WBC	Word Biblical Commentary
WTJ	The Westminster Theological Journal
Bib	*Biblica*
BJRL	*Bulletin of the John Rylands Library*
ICC	International Critical Commentary
ISBE	*International Standard Bible Encyclopaedia*
JBL	*Journal of Biblical Literature*
JRT	*Journal of Religious Thought*
JSNT	*Journal for the Study of the New Testament*
JSNTSS	Journal for the Study of the New Testament Supplement Series
JTS	*Journal of Theological Studies*
MA	Massachusetts
NavPress	Navigators Press
NICNT	New International Commentary on the New Testament
NIGTC	New International Greek Testament Commentary

NIV	The New International Version of the Bible (1973)
NRSV	The New Revised Standard Vers ion of the Bible (1989)
NSBT	New Studies in Biblical Theology
NTS	*Ne w Testament Studies*
RTR	*The Reformed Theological Review*
SAP	Sheffield Academic Press
SEÅ	Svensk exegetisk årsbok
SNTSMS	Society for New Testament Studies Monograph Series
TDNT	*Theological Dictionary of the New Testament*, eds G. Kittel and G. Friedrich, translated into English by G. W. Bromiley, 10 vols (Grand Rapids: Eerdmans, 1964–76)
TynBul	*Tyndale Bulletin*

Origins and Unresolved Tensions
Donald Robinson

Synopsis

The paper outlines the early development of a course in biblical theology at Moore college. The course arose from the influence of C. H. Dodd, Oscar Cullman and Gabriel Hebert on the author's own thinking about the nature of theological education. The seven-segment course was marked by the division of the biblical story into three distinct yet unified stages. The paper further reflects on issues such as mission in the New Testament, the relationship of Jew and Gentile and some of the 'loose' ends that require further exploration.

A personal account

I have been invited to say something about how a course in what became designated Biblical Theology was developed at Moore College in the 1950s, what influenced this development, how the subject was actually presented, and what may have been distinctive about the presentation. I would like also to indicate what seem to me now to have been some loose ends in the concept of biblical theology as it emerged from the course which evolved over about twenty years from its beginning.

The somewhat personal nature of the way I shall be telling this story is partly unavoidable. Some of my mode of telling also reflects the relative isolation of Australia from wider theological discourse in the period under review. Perhaps it may all be allowed under the guise of a minor exercise in local historical theology!

It was my privilege to be a member of the teaching staff of
Moore College during the last two years of the principalship of
T. C. Hammond (1952–53) and thereafter under both M. L.
Loane (1954–58) and D. B. Knox (from 1959 until 1972). In 1952
and for a few years thereafter there were only two full-time
teachers apart from the principal and vice-principal. All the
students were Anglican ordinands who prepared for the Licentiate in Theology examination of the Australian College of
Theology over a two-year period. My teaching subjects in this
connection were Church History (briefly), OT and Liturgiol-
ogy. However, an additional first year had been introduced at
the end of World War II to provide a foundation for the
Licentiate of Theology course, especially in biblical knowledge.
Students of Deaconess House also attended lectures in this
first-year course. One subject in that course was known as
Special Doctrine, which at that time was an introduction to the
biblical doctrine of the atonement.

Development of a course

When I was assigned by Principal Loane to teach Special Doctrine it was agreed that I would take the doctrine of the church
rather than of the atonement, as this had been the subject of my
own 'special doctrine' study in Part III of the Theological Tripos
at Cambridge a few years earlier. There was no prior thought
that I would develop a course in biblical theology, nor had it
occurred to me that there was such a discipline in the theological
curriculum. I must have been familiar with the term 'biblical
theology' being used in connection with the approach to the
message of the Bible to be found in the writings of people like
A. G. Hebert,[1] Norman Snaith,[2] or G. Ernest Wright.[3] But, although I appreciated what was coming from such scholars, I was
not a disciple in any particular school. I was a thoroughgoing
believer in the inspiration and integrity of the Bible as a whole,
and generally welcomed the emphasis on the essential unity of

---

[1] Eg *The Throne of David* (London: Faber, 1941).

[2] Eg *The Distinctive Ideas of the Old Testament* (London: Epworth Press, 1944).

[3] Eg *The Challenge of Israel's Faith* (London: SCM, 1946).

the Bible which was evident in writers like thos
was also aware of some convergence of conservativ
liberal attitudes (in terms of biblical scholarship) in thi
illustrated in R. V. G. Tasker's *The Old Testament in the*
Testament.[4] It is perhaps worth noting that Tasker had been
student under Sir Edwyn Hoskyns, whom Gabriel Hebert described as 'the great protagonist in England' of biblical theology,[5] and that Tasker, like Hebert, had been influenced by the
writings of Canon W. J. Phythian-Adams.[6]

But probably the strongest influence at that time on my own
thinking as to what gave the Bible theological coherence came
from C. H. Dodd. I had been much impressed with *The Parables*
of the Kingdom[7] and *The Apostolic Preaching and its Developments*[8]
even before I began my theological training, and at Cambridge
I had attended his lectures and his New Testament Seminar.
His *According to the Scriptures: The Sub-structure of New Testa-*
ment Theology[9] appeared about the time I began lecturing in
1952. Another book which influenced me formatively was
Oscar Cullman's *Christ and Time: The Primitive Christian Concept*
of Time and History.[10]

Such were some of the influences of which I was conscious
when I began to lecture in Special Doctrine. But it was especially
the idea of the church of God, or more precisely the people of

---

[4] First published in 1946 and again, fully revised, in 1954 (London: SCM). Tasker
moved increasingly to an evangelical position in theology. At London University
he was one of the teachers of Alan Cole, who taught at Moore College in 1952
(and at intervals thereafter). Alan Cole himself made a significant contribution
to biblical theology in his Tyndale New Testament Lecture of 1950 *The New*
Temple: A Study in the Origins of the Catechetical 'Form' of the Church in the New
Testament (London: Tyndale Press).

[5] *Fundamentalism and the Church of God* (London: SCM, 1957), 22.

[6] Eg *The Call of Israel: An Introduction to the Study of Divine Election* (Oxford, 1934):
The Fulness of Israel: A Study of the Meaning of Sacred History (Oxford, 1938).

[7] London: Nisbet, 1935.

[8] London: Hodder and Stoughton, 1936.

[9] London: Nisbet, 1952, based on the Stone Lectures given at Princeton Seminary in March 1950. I recall my friend Brevard Childs, whom I first met in North
America in 1947 and who went to Princeton as I went to Cambridge, writing to
tell me of the impact of these lectures.

[10] London: SCM, 1951. John Marsh's *The Fulness of Time* (London: Nisbet, 1952)
was also exploring this theme at that time.

God, which at that time for me gave coherence to the story of the Bible, and which led to the subject I chose for my Special Doctrine. My Cambridge supervisor, C. F. D. Moule, had drawn my attention to an older book with the title *The People of God*[11] by a Canadian scholar H. F. Hamilton, and I recall picking up a copy of it in Sydney in 1951. The significance of the covenant that God made with his people Israel was highlighted by many of the writers I have mentioned as being a crucial key to the structure of the biblical story, and this was reinforced by an article by James Packer on the pervasive presence of the covenant idea in Scripture, which appeared in the early stages of our course.[12]

One distinguished member of the 'biblical theology school' was in fact in Australia throughout the decade of the 1950s, and it is right to record the contact we at Moore had with him. Fr Gabriel Hebert of the Society of the Sacred Mission, author of the above-mentioned *The Throne of David*, was teaching at St Michael's House, Crafers, South Australia, from 1950 until 1961. I was in frequent contact with him after meeting him at a small conference of Evangelicals and Anglo-Catholics at St Paul's College in Sydney in 1952. We discussed many matters of biblical interpretation, as well as general questions of the nature of Scripture including its inspiration and infallibility. At the conference at St Paul's College, I had read a paper on 'The Evangelical Doctrine of Holy Scripture' to which he responded. His own mature view of biblical theology had recently been set out in his *The Bible from Within*.[13] It is not easy for me to trace any direct influence of his views on the contents of our course, although, as I shall show, we had a close affinity in one important feature of our hermeneutical principles. But there was an important aspect of his approach to theology and theological study which I did take note of and incorporated in our first-year course from an early stage. That aspect is set out in a lecture he gave to the

---

[11]   Vol. I Israel, Vol. II The Church (Oxford, 1912).

[12]   See further ' "The Church" Revisited: An Autobiographical Fragment', Donald Robinson, *Reformed Theological Review* Vol. 48/1. I would add to the books mentioned there, Alan Stibbs' *The Church Universal and Local* (London: Church Book Room Press, 1948), which I had read in England in 1950 and discussed with Alan Cole, who had been a tutor at Oak Hill Theological College with Stibbs.

[13]   Oxford, 1950.

Melbourne College of Divinity in July 1955.[14] The study of
theology, he urged, is engagement with God 'as living, real, and
active—as he has revealed himself'. In other words, God is
subject, and not merely object, for the student of theology.
Theology is indeed 'what we may rightly say about him', but
theological study is part of our discipleship as we prepare to
minister. The preparation of *ourselves* is as important as our
formal studies. We must come to terms with God in his word,
which means entering into the scriptural story. I incorporated
part of this lecture into my own lectures, and also devoted a
section to 'The character of God', which I admit was a piece of
systematic theologising based on the biblical evidence in
general.

In January 1957 Fr Hebert gave lectures to a Brisbane Clergy
School on 'Christ the Fulfiller: A study in Biblical Types'.[15] In
these he propounded an outline of the contents of the Bible in
three stages somewhat similar to that which I was developing
in the Moore College course. I shall say more about this when I
come to explain the contents of this course.

It is, however, appropriate to add here that some of us in
Australia were in discussion with Fr Hebert about the doctrine
of Scripture more or less continuously from 1952 to 1960. I have
mentioned the paper on 'The Evangelical Doctrine of Holy
Scripture', which he had taken up with me in 1952. His book
Fundamentalism and the Church of God was published by the SCM
Press in June 1957. It attracted wide attention and was replied to
in March 1958 by James Packer with his *'Fundamentalism' and the
Word of God* published by IVF.[16] Hebert was particularly critical
of the attitude of the Inter-Varsity Fellowship and its *New Bible*

---

[14] *Theology and Theological Study* (Sydney: Angus and Robertson. 1955).
[15] Sydney: Anglican Truth Society, 1957.
[16] Alan Cole had already replied to 'Gabriel Hebert on "Fundamentalism and
the Church of God" ' in *Reformed Theological Review* for February 1958. Though
trenchantly defending Conservative Evangelicalism—as distinct from Fundamentalism—against Hebert's criticisms, he says: '. . . we would find ourselves in
total agreement with most of what Fr Hebert has said about the nature and
meaning of Biblical "truth". We are of one mind: and our sphere of agreement
goes even further when Dr Hebert sees that the historicity of God's saving acts
as well as of their interpretation is essential, for if one is the warp of revelation,
then the other is the woof'. 20.

Commentary to Scripture. Some of us at Moore were fairly closely associated with the IVF. I myself was in the vulnerable position of being the IVF's commentator on *Jonah*! Hebert thought the *New Bible Commentary* was weak and timid in exegesis, that it lacked a full world view, an integrated biblical theology, and an adequate view of the church. My point in rehearsing all this is that our Biblical Theology course was being fashioned in the midst of an on-going debate with Dr Hebert himself—of a most charitable and constructive kind, I should say—on these very questions. In fact, some of the draft chapters of his book were submitted to some of us for comment before publication, and the Preface acknowledges 'conservative evangelical friends here in Australia . . . who have helped me much by the loan of books and in discussion'. This encounter certainly made me more sensitive than I might otherwise have been to the context in which the search for the theology of the Bible needed to be conducted. Having said that, I do not think there was ever any danger of our brand of conservative evangelicalism espousing a use of Scripture which took statements or verses out of their biblical contexts, which was alleged to be a characteristic of Fundamentalism. Hebert fully recognised that the hermeneutical principles we were expounding at Moore were taking proper account of the Bible's own structure. It is appropriate to mention, too, that in his discussion of the doctrine of Scripture itself Dr Hebert wrote appreciatively of Archdeacon T. C. Hammond's booklet *Inspiration and Authority*.[17]

Before looking at what was meant by biblical theology in the course actually devised and taught in the first year at Moore in the 1950s and 60s, it should be made clear that, notwithstanding the atmosphere of thought and debate I have just described, the course itself was a simple introductory course for new students looking towards the Anglican ministry. The aim was to assist them in their approach to theological study in general, and to the study of the Bible in particular. It began by asking what was the nature of the Christian ministry, and why certain subjects

---

[17] *Fundamentalism and the Church of God*, 60. I recall his writing to me after he had come across T. C. Hammond's *In Understanding Be Men* and commenting: 'a real theologian!'. Some lively and very good-humoured discussions took place between Hammond and Hebert during visits by the latter to Moore College.

were included in the college curriculum. A distinction was drawn between the study of the Christian religion in its various aspects (including credal doctrines, church history, Prayer Book) and the study of the Bible in its own terms to discover what it is all about. The practical intention of the course was stated as being 'to stimulate the student's general reading of the Bible'. There was a certain tension here. While there were a number of 'givens' in the theological curriculum, we were entering the Bible on a journey of exploration and discovery, without knowing what it would tell us. It would speak for itself, whether or not we knew what to do with it in the end. My job, I used to say, was to land the students on the moon: they might have to find their own way back to earth!

A description of the course

In its earlier years, under the broad title of 'An introduction to the study of the theology of the Bible' there were four segments:

a. The nature of theology and the Bible
b. The dominant themes of the Bible, especially the people of God and the covenant
c. The sacraments as covenant instruments
d. Principles of biblical interpretation.

As I have indicated, there was some preliminary skirmishing related more to the college course as a whole than to this particular subject. We discussed the purpose of the college and the scope of its curriculum, including the relation of systematic or dogmatic theology to biblical theology, and the relation of both to pastoral theology.[18]

By the end of my time, this preliminary discussion was followed by an expanded presentation in seven segments:

1. The character of the Bible: its scope and structure. This included an outline of the Bible's historical scope and spread,

---

[18] In later years I drew on Martin Thornton's *The Function of Theology* (London: Hodder and Stoughton, 1968), and especially his definition of pastoral theology as the drawing out of the practical implications of revelational theology— whether expressed biblically or dogmatically—in ministering to the Christian flock or individual.

and, although we did not speak much about the canon of
Scripture as such, we used the basic canonical categories of
'the law and the prophets' and 'the gospel and the apostle'.
Without embarking on literary criticism, we drew attention
to different literary genres and the need to be aware of
writers' intentions.

2. The people of God. This theme was identified as prominent
   and pervasive, and as central to God's response to the human
   condition. Associated with it are the various 'covenants' God
   made with those whom he chose. Covenants in general were
   examined, and then the particular features of those made
   with Noah, Abraham, and Israel at Mt Sinai.

3. The significance of 'Abraham and his seed'. God's promise
   to 'bless' Abraham was seen as the hope of 'salvation', and
   the whole biblical story as the outworking of that promise. It
   was fulfilled historically, via the redemption and exodus
   from Egypt, in the possession and enjoyment of the land of
   Canaan, reaching its climax in the kingdom of David and the
   son of David, Solomon.

4. The particular features of the two great episodes: exodus/
   redemption, and land/inheritance. Each has its cluster of
   incidents and symbols. The Exodus includes judgments on
   Pharaoh, the passover, passage of the sea, the manna, the rock
   and the cloud, the theophany and engagement with God at
   Sinai, the covenant, the law, the tabernacle, priesthood and
   worship: the trials and victories. The Land incidents include
   the crossing of Jordan, the conquest of Jericho, the allotting
   of inheritance, the kingship (God's rule), David, Jerusalem,
   full conquest and dominion over the land, the peace, glory
   and wisdom of Solomon, the temple, all peoples and all kings
   come to Solomon.

5. The prophets' view of promise and fulfilment in the period
   of decline and collapse of the historical experience of salvation in the land and in the subsequent exile. Their projection
   of the themes of Exodus (a new redemption) and the Land (a
   new inheritance, a new David, Jerusalem, and temple) into
   the coming 'day of the Lord'.

6. The NT claim that all this is fulfilled in Christ. The use of the
   Exodus and Land themes, and their attendant features, to

explain the work of Christ. Also, the tension within the NT between what was already fulfilled and what remained to be fulfilled in a yet future—though imminent—day of the Lord; the tension between the 'now' and the 'not yet'.

7. Principles of biblical interpretation. Based on the foregoing understanding of what the Bible is 'about', we enunciated a biblical 'typology' using the three stages in the outworking of God's promise to Abraham, that is, (a) the historical experience of the fulfilment of God's promise to Abraham through the exodus to the kingdom of David's son in the land of inheritance, (b) the projection of this fulfilment into the future day of the Lord, by the prophets, during the period of decline, fall, exile and return, and (c) the true fulfilment in Christ and the Spirit in Jesus' incarnation, death, resurrection, exaltation and in his parousia as judge and saviour in a new heaven and new earth.

The three-stage division

Perhaps the most distinctive feature of the foregoing concept of biblical theology was the division of the biblical story into three stages between Abraham and the parousia of Christ, ie from the promise to Abraham to the realisation of the promise in the kingdom of Solomon: from the decline of the kingdom to the end of the period of the prophets: and from the coming of Christ to the consummation of the age, or the period of the NT. The old-style Dispensationalists had various ways of dividing the Bible into periods. The seven dispensations of the Scofield Reference Bible,[19] for instance, were designated as 'the ordered ages which condition human life on the earth'.[20] From the call of Abraham to the giving of the law (Exodus 19:8) is the Dispensation of Promise, and from the giving of the law to Calvary is the Dispensation of Law. This is followed by the

---

[19] This was an edition of the Authorised Version 'with a new system of connected topical references to all the greater themes of Scripture . . .' C. I. Scofield, *Scofield Reference Bible* (London: Oxford University Press), 1917. It was familiar to many Australian evangelicals, not least when its sale was subsidised by a Sydney businessman prominent among the Brethren.

[20] See the Scofield note at Ephesians 1:10.

Dispensation of Grace and then, at the return of Christ, the
Dispensation of the Kingdom when the covenant with David
is realised. However, I do not think this kind of Dispensation-
alism had any influence in the circles that were looking for
biblical structures in the 1940s and 1950s. I think my own
awareness of the climactic significance of Solomon's kingdom
was due to three observations:

1. the terms of the revelation God gave to David concerning his
    son in 2 Samuel 7;
2. the sheer 'glory' of Solomon and his kingdom as described at
    length in 1 Kings 3 to 10, including the homage he received
    from all the people and kings of the earth and his own
    blessing the Lord 'that he hath given rest unto his people
    Israel, according to all that he promised: there hath not failed
    one word of all his good promise, which he promised by the
    hand of Moses his servant' (1 Kgs 8:56): and
3. Psalm 72, 'Of Solomon', which also celebrates Solomon's
    reign in superlative terms, concluding with a reference to
    God's promise to Abraham that 'all men shall be blessed in
    him', implying that the king is Abraham's seed (cf Gal 3:16)
    and the focus of blessing to the world.

Although not initially aware of anything in the biblical theologians quite like the three-fold division I was proposing, it was
some comfort to find that Gabriel Hebert had a somewhat
similar division in his *Christ the Fulfiller*, which he also set out in
his chapter on 'The Bible and God's Saving Purpose' in his
Fundamentalism and the Church of God in 1957.[21] Hebert's consequent idea of biblical typology was also congenial. We may
not read any symbolic meaning we like into biblical incidents or
features. Rahab's scarlet cord, which secured her salvation at
Jericho, has been taken, since Clement of Rome, as a type of the
blood of Christ, by which we are saved from destruction. It is
not unedifying, but it is arbitrary and gratuitous. The true

---

[21] Hebert's presentation of the 'Main Story' of the Bible in terms of three
'Confessions of Faith' relative to successive periods within that Story is appar-
ently derived from W. J. Phythian-Adams. *The Way of At-one-ment: Studies in
Biblical Theology* (London: Oxford University Press, 1944). See Hebert, *Christ the
Fulfiller*, 17.

biblical types are those 'which appear first in the narratives, and then re-appear in the prophetic hopes of God's future salvation, and are duly taken up in the New Testament fulfilment'.[22] This hermeneutical principle was identical with what our Biblical Theology course was using.

It will be apparent from the foregoing description of the early Biblical Theology course that the NT end of the treatment was slight compared with the handling of the OT. In truth it consisted of not much more than a drawing of attention to the various terms from, and allusions to, the OT which appear in the NT by way of explanation of Jesus' person and work. The course did little more than point out what lay behind such references to Jesus as 'fulfilling his exodus,[23] or as 'our passover',[24] or 'the bread from heaven',[25] or 'that rock',[26] or 'the living water',[27] or as 'tabernacling among us',[28] or as offering his 'blood of the covenant' to his disciples,[29] or as the giver of 'rest',[30] or as 'the son of David',[31] or as 'something greater than Solomon'[32] or 'greater than the temple'.[33] We did, however, look at the language of fulfilment—'the time is fulfilled'[34]—and were aware of the need to explicate the eschatological tension within the NT between the hour that 'is coming' and the hour that 'now is'.[35] This tension was much under discussion among scholars in terms like 'realised eschatology' and 'inaugurated eschatology'. The 1950s saw a spate of theological studies on the Christian hope.[36] While the course did not provide a very extensive treatment of this aspect, I did require the

---

22 Hebert. *Christ the Fulfiller*, 8.
23 Luke 9:31.
24 1 Cor 5:7.
25 John 6:33.
26 1 Cor 10:4.
27 John 4:10; 7:38.
28 John 1:14.
29 Mark 14:24.
30 Matt 11:28.
31 Matt 21:9; 22:45.
32 Matt 12:42.
33 Matt 12:6.
34 Mark 1:15, Gal 4:4.
35 John 4:23.
36 See, for example. J. A. T. Robinson, *Jesus and His Coming* (London: SCM, 1957) and the bibliography he gives on pages 9 and 13.

students to read the booklet *The Hope of Christ's Coming*,[37] which contained addresses I had given in the college chapel and which represented part of the thinking which belonged to an exploration of biblical theology.

But there was, as it happened, one partial elaboration of the fulfilment theme in the NT within the course, though only for a few years. This was a segment on the biblical basis of missions, and it came about in this way. About 1964, prior to the establishment of St Andrew's Hall in Melbourne as a training centre for Church Missionary Society candidates, the Federal Council of the Society asked Moore College to provide a preparatory course for such candidates. As part of such a course it was decided to extend the Biblical Theology course to take account of evangelisation and the spread of the gospel in relation to the fulfilment theme of the NT. This provided the opportunity to extrapolate a doctrine of missions or missionary activity from the pattern of God's salvation for all nations as revealed in the Bible's theology. This meant examining the role of 'the nations' both in the Bible's prologue (Genesis 1–11) and in the scope of the Abrahamic blessing, including the historical fulfilment in the reign of Solomon when 'all the earth sought the presence of Solomon to hear his wisdom which God had put in his heart' (1 Kgs 10:24) and when all kings paid homage to him and brought him presents. Then, how did the prophets project this 'proselyte' principle (ie Gentiles coming to the light) into the day of the Lord, and how is it fulfilled in the operation of the gospel of God through Jesus Christ in the NT? This latter involved an examination of the ministry of apostleship and its relation to both Israel and the Gentiles: the apostolic partnership of Galatians 2:9 and the recognition of Israel's *pneumatika* by the Gentile churches as set out in Romans 15:27.

Neither apostleship nor the relationship of Jews and Gentiles in the NT economy of salvation were new interests of mine when this missions segment was being devised. I had written on apostles and apostleship in the *Reformed Theological Review*

---

[37]   D. W. B. Robinson, *The Hope of Christ's Coming* (Sydney: Evangelical Tracts and Publications), 1955. Mention should also be made of John Bright's books, which were recommended to students at this time, especially *The Kingdom of God* (New York: Abingdon Press. 1955).

in 1954, and the relation of Jews and Gentiles was a growing interest in the 1950s; I had given the IVF Lecture on 'Jew and Greek: Unity and Division in the Early Church' in 1961 and further refined my views during study leave in Cambridge later that year. But the inclusion of a segment on missions in the Biblical Theology course necessitated an attempt to apply the biblical pattern to the present age, eg what is apostolic ministry today? and what is the role of a missionary society? The missions segment also compelled us to face the eschatological tension of the NT, as everything the NT says on the subject of mission or apostleship appears to be comprehended within the original apostolic generation, bounded by the parousia of Christ as the expectation and goal of that generation. The theology of mission as a component of the Biblical Theology course was of short duration in a formal way, but the discussion of the theology of evangelisation was to continue in a number of forms, prompted also, for example, by the Asia Evangelical Theological Consultation at Singapore in July 1970, in which I participated, and some of our biblical theology ideas found a place in such discussion.[38]

The relation of Jew and Gentile

It is not part of my brief to discuss the considerable critique of the biblical theology movement as a whole which has been offered over the last few decades,[39] or the work of Bill Dumbrell and Graeme Goldsworthy which has continued to develop biblical theology both within and beyond Moore College. If anyone is interested in my own thinking subsequent to my ceasing to have responsibility for the Biblical Theology course in the early 1970s, I would refer them to the Annual Moore College Lectures which I gave in 1981 under the title 'The Structure of New Testament

---

[38] See 'The Theology of Evangelism', a short paper read at the Asia Evangelical Theological Consultation, Singapore. by Donald Robinson, July 1970, published in *Interchange*, 3/1 (1971), 2–4.

[39] See, for example, Brevard Childs' *Biblical Theology in Crisis* (Philadelphia: Westminster Press, 1970) or Henning Graf Reventlow's *Problems of Biblical Theology in the Twentieth Century* (London: SCM, 1986).

Theology'.[40] The lecture on 'The Gospel and the Kingdom of God' contains a reflective summary of the approach to the Bible which had constituted the framework of our course, with the kingdom of God emerging as the dominant theme. The lecture on 'Jew and Gentile in the New Testament' is a direct consequence of my reading of biblical theology, and is specifically an attempt to correct what I consider to be a distortion of biblical truth which has persisted in Christian thinking from very early times:

> The popular view that God rejected the Jews and that the Gospel became a wholly Gentile matter Is so far at variance with the New Testament as well as with the expectation of the Old Testament that a complete reappraisal of the New Testament is called for.[41]

The question of the relation of Jew and Gentile in salvation history is one which rises directly from biblical theology, and is an unresolved tension among present-day theologians and Christian leaders. It has practical implications in connection with the establishment of the State of Israel and especially the claim that the land of Israel belongs to the Jews by divine covenant. Here, clearly, is a question for the biblical theologians! How much agreement is there among them? My own response to this precise question is set out in an article in *St Mark's Review* for Spring 1994 under the title 'Biblical understanding of Israel—the geographical entity: some prolegomena'.[42]

Loose ends revisited

In my opening words I spoke about 'loose ends'. The concept of biblical theology emerged almost unbidden from the introductory course on the Bible which began here in the 1950s. But our

---

[40] Published as *Faith's Framework* (Sydney: Albatross Books, 1985) and again by New Creation Publications: Blackwood, 1996. The lectures, I should add, are chiefly an attempt to see how the theology of the NT is related to the apostolic authority of the documents which comprise it, and to see what bearing this has on the principles of NT interpretation.

[41] Robinson, *Faith's Framework*, 97.

[42] Written for the International Affairs Commission of the General Synod of the Anglican Church of Australia, which was considering political and social implications of this issue.

treatment was far from exhaustive. One question could perhaps be put this way: Is the schema of the OT's 'promise and fulfilment', which is the framework of biblical theology as we have presented it, an adequate presentation of the Bible's message as a whole? Does it leave significant parts of the Bible unaccounted for? I believe the schema can be claimed as a plausible way of understanding or interpreting the main part of the OT, ie the law and the prophets (or, more exactly, the Torah, the former prophets, and the latter prophets of the Hebrew canon). But what of the rest of the OT, the writings? The second history, 1 Chronicles to Nehemiah, fits the schema well, but what of the other books? Some, like the Psalms and Proverbs, apparently attach themselves to the great figures of David and Solomon, but do they require special interpretation, and what do we make of apocalyptic on the one hand, or the story of Job on the other?

We are indebted to Graeme Goldsworthy for his wisdom regarding the place of wisdom in this connection, but let me say a word about the Psalms. Whatever else they do, they remind us that the OT pattern of promise, redemption, kingdom, etc was not play acting, not a charade. The experience of God which Israelites had was real for them, both as a nation and as individuals. The events may indeed have happened to them τνπικῶξ (figuratively?) as St Paul says,[43] and may have been recorded for our benefit ('upon whom the ends of the ages have come') rather than for theirs, but God was God, and faith and hope were real—so real that the Psalms have always been accepted by the Christian church as voicing the Christian response, individual and corporate, to all that God says to us in and through Christ. Thus we give our praise in the words of the Psalms for our creation, preservation, and all the blessings of this life, and, as well, for the redemption of the world by our Lord Jesus Christ. The whole biblical story becomes our own, from Abraham, through redemption in the exodus, the day of temptation in the wilderness, as pilgrims through this barren land, across the verge of Jordan to the promised land, and in the fruition of God's presence and rule in the prophetic hope of the city of God and of our dwelling in the house of the Lord for ever. I do not think

---

[43] 1 Cor 10:11

I made enough of the Psalms in the Biblical Theology courses. If I may use imagery David would not have understood, here is where the rubber hits the road. Here is the pastoral application of biblical theology. Despite the formal place of the Psalter in the liturgy of our church, its practical neglect in some of our churches is not a good sign for a true appreciation of biblical theology.

I referred earlier to the thinness of our original treatment of the NT in relation to the OT. To some extent it was possible for me to expand this in later stages of the college curriculum when I began to teach NT for the Licentiate in Theology in 1959, and more so when NT Theology became part of the college fourth-year curriculum. But there remains solid work to be done which would take account of books like N. T. Wright's *The New Testament and the People of God*[44] or G. B. Caird's posthumous *New Testament Theology.*[45]

Related to this question of the integration of the whole OT in the biblical theology schema is the manner in which the NT itself is used and interpreted in the modern church. The question which used to tease me was this: are we latter-day Christians to see ourselves as still within the Christian movement as depicted in the NT, still in the 'this is that'[46] era, still within the dynamics of Jew/Gentile relations, apostolic commissions, and expectations of the parousia of Christ in 'this generation', even though this generation has been unconscionably attenuated to now two millenia? Or are we to see ourselves as standing *outside* the whole biblical drama, from Abraham to parousia, accepting it as the divinely revealed paradigm in history of God's redemptive purpose for mankind, and, dare I say it, as providing the database, or mine of revelatory information, from which systematic theologians can draw the substance of their systematic constructions to comfort and enlighten Christians in their walk with God in this world?

I only say that this question used to tease me. I would put it to friends, who did not help me much! The Christian tradition to which we all belong has undoubtedly assumed and endorsed

---

44 London: SPCK, 1992.
45 Oxford: Clarendon, 1994.
46 Acts 2:16: 'this is that which was spoken by the prophet'.

the first answer as correct: we are still 'inside' the NT. On the other hand, that tradition has tended to act as if the *second* situation were the case! If the concept of biblical theology which I have been talking about provides a genuine understanding of the truth of God as it is revealed in Scripture, there is a lot of follow-up work yet to be done if its meaning and implications are to permeate our thinking, and the lives of our churches.

Exploring further

1. What do you regard as the advantages and disadvantages of Australia's relative isolation from wider theological discourse?
2. What is the relationship between inspiration and biblical theology?
3. Assess the value of the threefold structure of biblical revelation into
   (a) Abraham to Solomon
   (b) decline of the kingdom to the prophets
   (c) coming of Christ to the consummation.
4. Is 'promise and fulfilment' an adequate presentation of the Bible's message?
5. Are contemporary believers to see themselves 'inside' or 'outside' the biblical drama?

Is Biblical Theology Viable?
Graeme Goldsworthy

Synopsis

Biblical theology as a distinct discipline has come under close scrutiny in recent times. Many, including evangelicals, doubt its viability. Part of the problem is the lack of any agreed definition of 'biblical theology'. Some scepticism stems from historical and philosophical considerations while some is generated by the sheer size of the task of dealing with the Bible as a whole.

This paper examines the usefulness of beginning our investigation into biblical theology from three different points: the history of the name 'biblical theology'; the modern evangelical biblical theology movement; and the apostolic gospel. The first is unsatisfactory because of the lack of uniform understanding of what is involved, and because biblical theology as we now understand it began long before the name was coined. The second shows a vigorous pursuit of a way of looking at the Bible as a whole, but a failure to work out a consistent approach. A viable biblical theology is not only possible but demanded by the witness of Jesus and the apostles. It starts with the implications of the gospel for the unity of the Bible and takes its lead from the way the apostles preached Christ as the fulfilment of the OT.

Evangelical presuppositions concerning the Bible are taken as a starting point which must come under constant scrutiny. They are consistent with the emergence of a biblical theology which has apostolic authority, and which understands redemptive revelation in three stages following on the creation revelation of Eden. These three stages involve salvation revealed in Israel up to Solomon and the temple, a recapitulation of that revelation in prophetic eschatology, and the fulfilment in Christ.

Introduction: the challenge to viability

Recently I was a member of a consultative committee which was discussing the formation of a curriculum for theological training. I ventured the suggestion that a course in biblical theology would be appropriate. Another member of the committee, who has a PhD in NT, objected that the draft curriculum already contained such a course, and pointed to the doctrine segments.

In the discussion that followed it became clear to me that this person understood 'Biblical Theology' to mean theology that was in accord with the Bible in contrast with unbiblical (and therefore heretical) theology. That is a confusion that one continues to encounter. How, then, do we define biblical theology and, more importantly, is there such a discipline which is viable, useful, and valid?

The difficulties in arriving at an agreed definition of biblical theology should not deter us from proposing some kind of working definition which can then be finetuned if necessary. Negatively, there seems to be some agreement that biblical theology is theology that has not moved, beyond the forms in the Bible, to the formulation of Christian doctrine. On the positive side there is a recognition of some kind of unity in the Bible which attaches to its theology. Those who accept the validity of biblical theology also have broad agreement that it is concerned to describe the theology which is in the biblical books, and to do so in a way that reflects the theological methods or perspectives of the biblical authors.

To us who have come to think of biblical theology as an essential component of our biblical study, and as part of the necessary exegetical framework for understanding the message of the Bible, the notion that others, especially evangelicals, could have doubts about the viability of the discipline is almost unthinkable. Yet it is true that there are very different ideas about what biblical theology consists of. Furthermore, the widespread pastoral neglect of the subject results not only from ignorance of the apparent gains from employing it but also from a real

scepticism concerning the legitimacy of such an approach to the
Bible.

There are a number of possible reasons for such scepticism,
and these must be addressed if we are to persist in our belief that
biblical theology is essential to a good grasp of the Bible's
message and to a sound interpretation and application of the text
to our contemporaries. The problems in the doing of biblical
theology are well documented and widely discussed. For example, H. G. Reventlow focussed on the problem of the unity of the
Bible, and especially on the relationship between the two testaments.[1] Don Carson has referred to the main challenges to
biblical theology resulting from different presuppositions about
the text and the nature of revelation.[2] He also refers to the
methodological challenges in using the range of exegetical tools
over the whole Bible. Carson points us to the important problem
of an organising principle, which is probably one of the most
contentious issues in the contemporary debate. Finally there is
the question of how biblical theology relates to the formulation
of doctrine and to pastoral practice. I believe it is true to say that
all of these matters are only different expressions of the central
question of the nature and authority of Scripture.

David Adams points to three trends which threaten a genuine biblical theology.[3] The first is the refusal to engage with
theology as theology so that the biblical endeavour is reduced
to the history of religions. The second is the exclusive attention
to a diachronic approach to the text which excludes the synchronic or canonical approach.[4] The third is the tendency to see

---

[1] H. G. Reventlow, *Problems of Biblical Theology in the Twentieth Century* (Philadelphia: Fortress Press, 1986), 10–144. Translated from the German edition
published in 1983.

[2] D. A. Carson, 'Current Issues in Biblical Theology: A New Testament Perspective', *Bulletin for Biblical Research* (1995), 5.

[3] D. L. Adams, 'The Present God: A Framework for Biblical Theology', *Concordia
Journal*, (1996), 22.

[4] It should be noted that the terms 'diachronic' and 'synchronic' can be applied
in two distinct ways that easily cause confusion. When applied to the text, a
synchronic approach focuses on the text as it is in the canon, while the diachronic
attempts to penetrate the biblical text to its historical antecedents. The assumption here is often that it is the original saying or text which interests us rather
than the way it has grown and been adapted into its final form. It is this textual
evolutionism that Adams is criticising. By contrast, the synchronic approach
looks at the text as we have it in its canonical form. But when we apply these
terms to the theological concepts of the Bible, the synchronic approach asks about
the theology at any given point in time or of any given biblical author or corpus.

diversity without unity, to view the faith of Israel as polydox and polyphonic. These three tendencies have a long history stemming from the presuppositions of the Enlightenment and the historical-critical method. They touch the heart of the matter in that they challenge our view of Scripture as the inspired word of God.

Perhaps more serious for the evangelical theologian is the strenuous attack of James Barr on the whole way we do biblical theology, and especially on the idea of salvation-history.[5] Barr's attack focuses on the influence of neo-orthodoxy. He raises legitimate questions about the nature of history and of biblical history-writing which evangelical biblical theologians must take seriously. But these questions are not largely different from the ones which emerged with historical criticism and the consequent scepticism about what really happened. We have seen this debate carried on through a whole range of philosophical views. We cannot be satisfied with the existential approach of Bultmann, who seems indifferent to whether the events of biblical salvation-history actually took place. On the other hand, we are coming to recognise more that biblical historians did not necessarily operate with the same canons of historicity as modern historiography.

The challenges to the viability of biblical theology, then, are of two kinds: the theoretical or philosophical, and the practical. If this is the case, then the first step in resolving the legitimacy of our approach to biblical theology is to identify our presuppositions concerning Scripture. The second step is to try to understand how our presuppositions will affect the quest for a biblical theology. Thirdly, we need to question our presuppositions and whether they need some modification.

Before doing this, I will endeavour to contextualise the discussion by examining the implications of three starting points in our investigation of biblical theology. The first starting point is the history of the term 'biblical theology'. The second starting point

---

[4] *(continued)* through the biblical history. An evangelical biblical theology would favour a synchronic approach to the text while employing both synchronic and diachronic approaches to the theological content of the Bible.

[5] James Barr, *Fundamentalism* (London: SCM Press, 1977, 2nd ed 1981); 'Story and History in Biblical Theology', *Explorations in Theology*, 7 (1980), 1–17.

is the modern evangelical approach to the writing of biblical theology. Then I will consider a third starting point: a gospel-centred approach to biblical theology. My aim is to show that the historical studies are valuable but are not the grounds for an authentic and viable biblical theology. A gospel-centred approach alone will suffice as the basis of such a biblical theology.

The history of the name 'biblical theology' as our starting point

One starting point for this investigation is the origin of biblical theology as a self-conscious discipline and the use of the term as a way of designating a definable approach to the study of theology. This is problematical, since there is no reason why the term should be used in a consistent way, nor that the history of its usage should be tied to one identifiable approach. But at least we can explore the history of the name 'biblical theology' and see if it is productive.

Some surveys of the history of biblical theology start with J. P. Gabler and his inaugural lecture at Altdorf in 1787.[6] Gabler is important for making a distinction between biblical theology and dogmatic theology. But he was not the first to use the term 'biblical theology'. Hans-Joachim Kraus[7] notes the background of the Reformation dogma of *sola scriptura* as necessary for biblical theology to arise as a discipline. The title 'biblical theology' first occurred, according to Kraus,[8] in a 1629 work by Wolfgang Jacob Christmann. Then came the biblical theologies of Henricus Diest (1643) and Sebastian Schmidt (1671). These are characterised by the proof-texting of dogmas. The point about the Reformation background is that the Old and New Testaments were seen as sufficient for faith and salvation, contrary to the position of the Roman Catholic church. However, with time, biblical theology was also seen as a rejection of certain features of Protestant dogmatic theology.

---

[6] So, Wilfrid Harrington, *The Path of Biblical Theology* (Dublin: Gill and Macmillan, 1973), 19.

[7] *Die Biblische Theologie: Ihre Geschichte und Problematik* (Neukirchen-Vluyn: Neukirchener Verlag, 1970), 17.

[8] Kraus, 19, 20.

In the seventeenth century, Reformation covenant theology was given new impetus and shape with scholars like Coccejus, who saw God's revelation as a series of stages within the history of God's people. There is a possibility that Coccejus depended on the work of Georg Calixt (1654). The latter shows that in the seventeenth century there was an interest in what we refer to as salvation-history.[9]

The other dimension of the development of biblical theology was the pietist revolt against what was seen to be an increasingly sterile orthodox dogmatics. The so-called Protestant scholasticism was, according to Gerhard Ebeling, at least in part due to the failure to work through the implications of the Reformation's *sola scriptura*. Any tension between exegesis and dogmatics was excluded, because 'exegesis was enclosed within the frontiers fixed by systematic theology'.[10] Whether that is a fair assessment or the filtered interpretation of an Enlightenment thinker is not vital to our discussion. The pietists of the seventeenth century were certainly concerned about dogmatic orthodoxy, rightly or wrongly, and urged the need to distinguish between biblical theology and scholastic theology. Philip Jacob Spener's *Pia Desideria* (1675) is a case in point. Ebeling comments thus:

> For the understanding of the concept 'biblical theology' at the time of its origin the following point is significant: it is the slogan of a programme of theological reform which directed its criticism neither at the content of Orthodox dogmatics nor at its methodological form as systematic theology, but only at certain accretions, namely, at the fact that, as Spener says, there has been 'much introduced into theology which is alien, useless and savours more of the wisdom of the world'.[11]

According to Kraus, the influence of such Pietism in the writing of biblical theology is first seen in the *Biblische Theologie* of Carl Haymann (1708).

We see, then, that there are two initial considerations in the history of biblical theology: the driving force or forces, and the

---

[9] Kraus, 21.

[10] G. Ebeling, *Word and Faith* (Philadelphia: Fortress Press, 1963), 82.

[11] Ebeling, 84.

typical shape which develops into a salvation-history format.
Carl Friedrich Bahrdt's *Versuch eines biblischen Systems der Dog-
matik* (1770) was both a rejection of the 'complicated world of
scholastic theology' and an examination of the structure of divine revelation.[12] The question of the relationship of the testaments was posed in terms of the unity and the distinctions,
something, of course, that Calvin had dealt with over two hun-
dred years earlier.[13] Bahrdt distinguished four periods in OT
revelation: 1. from the fall to the flood; 2. from the flood to Moses;
3. from Moses to the Babylonian exile; and 4. from the exile to
Herod the Great. Ebeling presses the point that Pietism was
unable to draw from the concept 'biblical theology' the decisive
methodological consequences.[14]

For Ebeling it is the Enlightenment which provided an understanding of the consequences which saw biblical theology be-
coming the actual rival of dogmatics. This is not the rejection of
dogmatics but the setting up of biblical theology as an independent discipline justified in its own right. In this regard Gabler's inaugural address of 1787 is usually said to be important.
He proposed a distinction between biblical and dogmatic theology. His aim was to try to bring some unity into the theological
discussion, in which the variety of views of the orthodox, pietists, and rationalists bred confusion. He first distinguished
between the simple basic beliefs necessary for living life and for
salvation (religion) and the more complicated and abstract statements of theology.[15] The historical nature of biblical theology is
not a way of giving pre-eminence to history. History is secondary to what is true. As Sandys-Wunsch and Eldridge comment
on Gabler:

> The task of biblical theology is to work out what the truth
> contained in Scripture is. When he says that biblical theol-
> ogy is of historical origin, then, what he means is that

---

[12] Kraus, 28, 29.

[13] For example in his treatment of the relationship between the testaments in
Book II.10,11 of the *Institutes*.

[14] Ebeling, 86.

[15] J. Sandys-Wunsch and L. Eldredge, 'J.P. Gabler and the distinction between
biblical and dogmatic theology: Translation, commentary, and discussion of his
originality', SJT, 33 (1980), 133–158.

biblical theology by proper investigation of the documents in the Bible should aim at isolating their purely historical characteristics in order to eliminate them and leave the truth exposed. History on its own has no significance for biblical theology.[16]

Whether, as some suggest, Gabler was dependent on Gotthelf Traugott Zacharia[17] is not important for this discussion. What interests us is the points of agreement between the two:[18]

    i. Biblical theology must be more than a collection of proof texts.

    ii. The Bible is the divinely inspired means of guidance.

    iii. It must nevertheless be exegeted by sound methods.

    iv. Doctrines can be derived by comparing passages of Scripture.

    v. Some of the ideas in the Bible are attributable to the more primitive outlook of the writers.

But there are also points of difference. Gabler was more a product of the Enlightenment and could not assume the compatibility of revelation and reason. Gabler needed to justify dogmatics, which he did by his distinction between religion and theology. Both were legitimate. The problem of Scripture, however, still had to be dealt with. He finally made a distinction between biblical religion as it appeared in history (which he called 'true biblical theology') and a biblical theology which set out eternal truths enclosed in history (which he called 'pure biblical theology').[19] Thus, Gabler made a three-fold distinction between true biblical theology, pure biblical theology, and dogmatics. It could be argued that his main concern was not to establish biblical theology as such, but to rescue dogmatics from increasing confusion.[20]

---

[16] Sandys-Wunsch and Eldredge,147.

[17] *Biblische Theologie oder Untersuchung des biblischen Grundes der vornehmsten theologischen Lehren* (1771).

[18] Sandys-Wunsch and Eldredge, 152.

[19] Sandys-Wunsch and Eldredge, 157 and footnote 1: 'Later Gabler came to describe this as the difference between *wahre* and *reine* biblical theology.'

[20] See John Hayes and Frederick Prussner, *Old Testament Theology: Its History and Development* (Atlanta: John Knox Press, 1985), 62–66.

The effect of the Enlightenment on the course of biblical theology must not be confused with the essence and viability of biblical theology. Gabler's attempt to establish the validity of both biblical and dogmatic theology raises the important question of the relationship of the two. The answer to this question is dependent on how the two theological disciplines are perceived and how the source of revelation in Scripture is understood. If biblical theology is conceived of as purely descriptive and historical, it will reject, in all probability, any dogmatic principles that might define its method or limits. The question then arises as to whether a biblical theology leaves any room at all for dogmatics. However, once it is recognised that presuppositions play their foundational part in shaping exegesis and theological method, the question becomes a philosophical-theological one of the nature of such presuppositions.

The cleavage of biblical theology into the two disciplines of OT theology and NT theology is as regrettable as it was inevitable. It might be argued that it was inevitable purely on the grounds of division of labour. As biblical studies developed more and more specialities it was simply not possible for one person to be a specialist in the whole Bible. It is more likely, however, that the cleavage was due to the attack on the canon as the authoritative source of revelation. According to Wilfrid Harrington, the first biblical theology written according to Gabler's principles was the *Theology of the Old Testament* of G. L. Bauer (1796).[21] It is clear that the unity of the Bible was by then not well defended by orthodox dogma, nor by the concept of a canon of inspired Scripture.

In time, the development of historical criticism on the basis of Enlightenment presuppositions led to the rejection of the notion of revelation, and biblical theology became absorbed into the study of the history of religious ideas in the Bible. The historical philosophy of Hegel gave rise to the idea of religious evolution, so that, for example, W. Vatke in his *Religion des AT* (1835) distinguished the pre-prophetic, the prophetic, and the post-prophetic periods in Israel in terms of simple and primitive notions developing into more complex and sophisticated ones.

---

[21] Harrington, 20.

This evolutionary approach was later developed by Graf and Wellhausen.[22]

The history of religions movement thrived on historical criticism. The twentieth century saw a resurgence of activity in the writing of OT and NT theologies, but almost no biblical theologies. Pietism and a tenacious orthodoxy had persevered during the ascendancy of the history of religions movement in the nineteenth century. There are at least three dimensions to the twentieth-century scene. Firstly, traditional or evangelical orthodoxy continued to maintain pre-Enlightenment presuppositions to the doing of theology. This is not to say that conservative writers were completely preserved from the effects of the Enlightenment, nor that they completely ignored the gains of the new critical methods. But orthodoxy maintained that the presuppositions of biblical study were themselves revealed in the Bible. Secondly, the methods of the critical theologians underwent some changes, and different questions were being asked from those of the early historical-critical liberalism. Thirdly, neo-orthodoxy questioned the whole structure of Enlightenment thinking and allowed theological questions again to be asked of the biblical text.

According to Brevard Childs[23] the modern, especially the American, biblical theology failed to come to terms with the authority of Scripture. Ironically, Childs' canonical approach has not produced a viable biblical theology for the very same reason.[24] Childs' contribution could easily occupy a whole paper or, indeed, a whole school of theology. Yet, without wanting to take away from his achievement, it has to be said that from an evangelical point of view he has not really recovered a biblical method. At best he has pointed a way back to doing theology on

---

[22] O. Betz, 'Biblical theology, history of.' IDB (New York: Abingdon Press, 1962), 418–37.

[23] *Biblical Theology in Crisis* (Philadelphia: Westminster, 1970), 53.

[24] *Biblical Theology of the Old and New Testaments* (London: SCM, 1992). This volume of over 700 pages is a mine of information and contains a very useful section of prolegomena. But when it comes to the content of biblical theology, it would seem that Childs' canonical approach is not robust enough to allow him to draw the various traditions of the Scriptures together into any recognisable unity. He is so busy chasing various 'trajectories' (a word he uses *ad nauseam*) that he seems to miss the significance of the apostolic view of the one story.

the Bible's own terms but has not extended canonical shape to canonical authority.

As a postscript to this section I propose that the practical separation of the testaments is a serious challenge to the viability of biblical theology. A theology of the OT or a theology of the NT is not a biblical theology, however much there may be a convergence of methods employed by each. This is not to criticise the contributions of those who have written in each field, but only to lament the fact that modern scholarly standards have contributed to the feeling that no-one is clever enough or can live long enough to write a biblical theology on the whole of the canon. The twentieth century has seen the production of many theologies of either testament but very few attempts at a theology of both testaments. This has highlighted the problem of the relationship between the testaments and, one might suggest, led to various kinds of distortion in scholarly perspectives on the Bible. The danger of such distortion for the NT theologian is arguably less than for the OT theologian. This is because NT theologians have as their primary sources documents which clearly understand themselves in relation to the OT and constantly refer to it.

The OT theologian who writes from within a Christian tradition may adopt an approach which is more or less focussed on some concept of a relationship with what emerges in the NT. It is interesting how some OT theologians have included prefaces or excursuses setting out the need to understand the OT in relation to the New and then seem to ignore totally their own advice (for example, Eichrodt, von Rad, Vriezen).[25]

It must be concluded that the name 'biblical theology' does not lead us to a definitive concept of a viable discipline. On the one hand, we must accept that biblical theology has been around considerably longer than the title and, on the other hand, we see that the name has been used to apply to a whole range of different approaches. These have largely been marked by different philosophical starting points. May we propose, then, that those who share the same basic evangelical understanding of the

---

[25] An exception to this is the self-consciously Christian work of G.A.F. Knight, *A Christian Theology of the Old Testament* (London: SCM Press, 1959).

nature and authority of the Bible will provide a more authentic starting point?

The Modern Evangelical Biblical Theology Movement[26] as our starting point

As a student at Moore College in the mid-fifties, I was introduced to biblical theology primarily through two books and through a lecture given by the then vice principal, Donald Robinson. The two books were John Bright's *The Kingdom of God* (1955)[27] and Geerhardus Vos's *Biblical Theology Old and New Testaments* (first published 1948).[28] Later, Edmund Clowney's *Preaching and Biblical Theology* (1961)[29] reinforced much of what I had learnt from these others.

John Bright: *The Kingdom of God*

Bright's book is a biblical theology in that it retells the biblical story through the eyes of a historian who is a theologian and a believer. It takes a thematic approach dictated by the gospel witness to the kingdom of God and traces that idea through the whole Bible. Bright's critical presuppositions show in that he begins the OT story with Israel in the promised land.[30] The historian's concern for the recovery of what lay behind the

---

[26] I use the term 'movement' loosely, though not without justification. As an evangelical movement, it predates the so-called American biblical theology movement, which was largely driven by neo-orthodoxy.

[27] English edition: J. Bright, *The Kingdom of God in Bible and Church* (London: Lutterworth, 1955).

[28] G. Vos, *Biblical Theology Old and New Testaments* (Grand Rapids: Wm. B. Eerdmans, 1948).

[29] Edmund Clowney, *Preaching and Biblical Theology* (Grand Rapids: Wm. B. Eerdmans, 1961).

[30] Bright's prolegomenon to *A History of Israel* is the monograph *Early Israel in Recent History Writing* (London: SCM Press, 1956). Bright's case, as he argues it against Martin Noth, is essentially that we can have reasonable confidence in the biblical documents as historical records. However, he argues on the basis of probability rather than of a doctrine of Scripture. It would appear that he adopts much the same presuppositions as Noth but does not share the latter's scepticism about the records of early Israel.

documents does not allow the theologian in him to deal with the
patriarchs and the exodus other than as Israel's memory. The
strength of Bright's book is the sense of the unity of Scripture
and its testimony to the coming of the kingdom of God. He
writes with warm piety and pastoral concern, but he cannot be
said in either *The Kingdom of God* or his *The Authority of the Old
Testament*[31] to represent an evangelical position on the nature
and authority of Scripture.

Geerhardus Vos: *Biblical Theology Old and New Testaments*

Geerhardus Vos lectured and wrote from a position of Reformed
orthodoxy. His work has had a great influence among Reformed
Protestant theological students, certainly of my generation. Vos
did two things for us: he gave us a clear, if brief, statement of the
principles and method of biblical theology, and gave us an
example of how the task should be done. Vos's *Biblical Theology
Old and New Testaments* has some curious weaknesses. While it
is useful to have his interactions with the various critical positions of his day, and his treatments of revelation and the nature
of prophecy, these would have been better placed in a prolegomenon. But worse, Vos virtually ignores the whole of the
former prophets and moves from Mosaic revelation to the latter
prophets. In so far as Samuel and Kings appear in the book, it is
in the section dealing with the nature of the prophetic office.
Thus the whole theology of the former prophets is missing as is
the wisdom literature.

Even more extraordinary is Vos's treatment of the NT. While
there are some brief references to the Acts and the epistles,
these are in the context of the ministry of Jesus. But, even here,
there is a sudden halt to the work with the life of Jesus. The
death, resurrection and ascension are not noted even in the
index. Now, Vos died in 1949, the year after his biblical theology, edited by his son, was published. But there are no indications given by either editor or publisher that illness or
impending death was what caused the book to be unfinished.

---

31 John Bright, *The Authority of the Old Testament* (London: SCM Press, 1967).

Vos's inaugural lecture as Professor of Biblical Theology at Princeton Seminary, 1894,[32] gives a better indication of where he could have taken his work in a comprehensive and Christ-centred way. Here he defines biblical theology as: 'that part of Exegetical Theology which deals with the revelation of God in its historic continuity'.[33] Stressing the historical element, Vos goes on to define biblical theology as, *the exhibition of the organic progress of supernatural revelation in its historic continuity and multiformity*'.[34] Whatever defects we might find in Vos's work, his inaugural lecture is in stark contrast with that of one of his successors, J. C. Beker, whose inaugural address as Professor of Biblical Theology at Princeton was given in 1968.[35] Beker seemed more concerned to castigate biblical theology than to promote and commend it.

But the failure of Vos to finish his best-known work is not, in my opinion, as significant as the defects in his actual analysis of the OT revelation. Anyone can see the work is incomplete. It is more difficult to critique what is there. His introduction sets out certain principles, starting with the presupposition of God and his revelation. One such principle is that of periodicity, or the recognition of epochs in biblical revelation. Yet Vos gives no real explanation for his omission of the substantial epoch of the former prophets. When he comes to the latter prophets his treatment is more in the format of a systematic theology: attributes of God, covenant, sin, and restoration. This tends to be done without reference to the significance of the ongoing historical process, and little, if anything, is made of the different perspectives of pre-exilic, exilic, and post-exilic prophecy. I would conclude that Vos has not been as successful as we might wish in carrying out his own principles.

---

[32] Reproduced in Richard B. Gaffin, Jr., (ed.) *Redemptive History and Biblical Interpretation, The Shorter Writings of Geerhardus Vos* (Phillipsburg: Presbyterian and Reformed, 1980), 3–24.

[33] Gaffin, 10.

[34] Gaffin, 15 (italics his).

[35] J.C. Beker, 'Biblical Theology in a Time of Confusion', *Theology Today*, 25/2, (1968), 185–94. Beker, like Barr, rejects the notion of salvation-history and accuses one of its main exponents, Oscar Cullmann of philosophical-theological naivete.

Edmund Clowney: *Preaching and Biblical Theology*

Edmund Clowney follows in Vos's footsteps and shows some developments and refinements. He defines the redemptive-historical development in terms of the periods marked by creation, the fall, the flood, Abraham, the exodus, and the advent. He does not explain why he would use these parameters, nor how the designated epochs relate. Everybody recognises that there is development in the biblical message, and listing a series of significant events and people is hardly profound. Periodicity is not the issue. The issue is whether or not the various parts can be said to hang together in some kind of meaningful whole, and, if they do, what kind of unity they form. The same weakness, it seems to me emerges in Clowney's more recent book *The Unfolding Mystery*.[36]

Willem VanGemeren: *The Progress of Redemption*

Amore recent work of biblical theology is Willem VanGemeren's *The Progress of Redemption* (1988).[37] This author indicates his indebtedness to both Vos and Clowney. His epochal analysis involves twelve periods of redemptive history: creation; fall; election and promise; a holy nation (Exod – Josh); a nation like other nations (Judg – 1 Sam 15); a royal nation (1 Sam 16 – 1 Kgs 11); a divided nation (1 Kgs 12 – 2 Kgs 25); a restored nation (Ezra, Neh, prophets); Jesus and the kingdom; apostolic era; the kingdom and the church. Now there is no doubt that these epochs exist, though it is not clear what the significance of 'epoch' is seen to be. VanGemeren's presuppositions include the acceptance of the Bible as the word of God and the word of man, and the recognition that the theological centre of the Bible is Jesus Christ. He indicates that the redemptive-historical significance of the various epochs

---

[36] Edmund Clowney, *The Unfolding Mystery* (Leicester: IVP, 1988). To be fair to the author it must be said that this is not strictly a biblical theology. It is a popularly and, it must said, warmly written book with the subtitle, *Discovering Christ in the Old Testament*. Nevertheless, Clowney's biblical theological concern is evident throughout.

[37] Willem VanGemeren, *The Progress of Redemption* (Grand Rapids: Academie Books, 1988).

must be seen in the light of Jesus Christ. The twelve periods are 'convenient dividers along the long road of redemptive history'.[38] He admits that the number twelve is arbitrary. It appears that they are chosen, not for any organic or theological reason, but because they constitute a convenient succession of stages leading to the culmination in Christ.

The epochal structure of redemptive history is more than a convenient way of handling a large corpus, as I'm sure VanGemeren would agree. But it appears that his method does not take sufficient account of his own principles, and especially that of the centrality of Jesus Christ. Biblical theology is not a matter of carving the Bible into manageable chunks and then investigating how the various parts relate to one another and especially to the coming of Christ. If VanGemeren's presuppositions are sustainable, and I firmly believe they are, then the gospel must be taken as the guide to the essential, as against convenient, epochal structure of the canonical revelation. How did Jesus and the apostles see the epochs and the progressive stages of redemptive history? In other words, if the Bible has a real theological unity while being a progressive record of redemptive revelation, the epochs should help us to relate the parts to the whole in a way that reveals more than a sequence of people and events. It must yield interpretative principles.

There are other evangelical works that we could consider which are specifically concerned with either OT theology or NT theology.[39] Our concern here is with biblical theology which, by definition, deals with the whole Bible. Theologies of either testament have made important contributions to biblical studies, and some have opened up the question of biblical-theological method in a significant way. But the downside is that the splitting of the

---

[38] VanGemeren, 32.

[39] For example, E.A. Martens, *Plot and Purpose in the Old Testament* (Leicester: IVP, 1981); W.C. Kaiser, *Toward an Old Testament Theology* (Grand Rapids: Zondervan, 1962); G.E. Ladd, *A Theology of the New Testament* (Grand Rapids: Eerdmans, 1974). These, and many others, employ varieties of biblical-theological method, but they are, by definition, not biblical theologies. I would go further to say that, whatever the benefits of the many theologies of either testament, the tendency to split the Bible into two sections which are dealt with separately has not served the cause of biblical theology well.

canon has become more than a matter of specialisation and division of labour. It has in practical terms become the actual hermeneutical divide in so much that passes for Christian teaching and
preaching.

We must ask why evangelical biblical theologians, who start
with essentially the same presuppositions about the Bible,
produce such a wide diversity of approaches. One possibility
is that the nature of the biblical data is such that it allows such
diversity. Another possibility is that the implications of our
doctrine of Scripture have yet to be worked out in relation to
biblical theological method. It is to this latter concern that I now
turn.

The gospel as our starting point

An evangelical approach to biblical theology (or to any kind of
theology for that matter) must begin with the person of Jesus
Christ. Some would argue that we must begin with the Bible as
the word of God inscripturate since that is our only source of
knowledge of Jesus as the Word of God incarnate. Both views
have validity. It is the Christ of the Bible who meets us in his
gospel and converts us from being the enemies of God to being
his friends. Let us accept for the moment the presuppositions
that God is there, and that he has spoken by the prophets in the
OT and, latterly, by his Son in the NT (Heb 1:1,2).

The biblical testimony to Jesus has many implications for the
way we understand the Bible.

   i. Jesus is declared to be the truth who makes God
      known. He is the God-man who makes God known in
      relation to sinners as the gracious, saving God.
  ii. This same incarnated Word, Jesus, breaks the vicious
      cycle of humankind's rebellion against God, being
      given over by God to this state of rebellion and conse-
      quent judgment. He is the truth, not simply the infor-
      mation giver. Human beings need more than
      information about God. The race is in deep moral
      revolt against God, and, if it is to benefit from special
      revelation, it must be a redemptive word that God
      speaks.

iii. God does not speak a variety of different words. The word of the prophets (OT) and the word of the Son (NT) are one word. Moreover, without ever ignoring the important distinctions between them, we must say that the word inscripturate (canon of Old and NTs) and the Word incarnate (Jesus) are the same word. The most important distinction is that the Word incarnate is the living God whom we worship, while the word inscripturate is an inspired collection of books which we do not worship.[40] What is often ignored by those who use slogans such as, 'God does not reveal propositions but himself', is that the distinction thus made is meaningless. Without the word inscripturate we cannot know the Word incarnate nor the God revealed in the Word himself. It is curious how some scholars are so keen to assert by propositions that God cannot, or will not, communicate propositionally.

iv. The one word of God centres on the gospel event, the life death and resurrection of Jesus of Nazareth. The word of the prophets testifies to this one redemptive event. The constant testimony of the NT is that the Word incarnate claims to sum up the prophetic word. The Word incarnate and the word inscripturate are distinguishable but inseparable.

It is here that we must remind ourselves of our presuppositions. These can be of different orders and be expressed in a variety of ways. We will rarely feel constrained to try to enunciate an absolute starting point in metaphysical terms. We assume that such a starting point, or something like it, would be universally accepted. Wherever we do focus on our assumptions they must always be open to question. It is not a matter of an arbitrary choice which none may query. We do our best to identify the working presuppositions which we apply in any endeavour, and to submit them to regular scrutiny. Presuppositions may be questioned as to what prior presuppositions they imply,

---

[40] The accusation often made against evangelicals, and even more often against fundamentalists, that these positions involve bibliolatry is not in accord with the facts. Both of these groups would recognise clearly the distinctions mentioned.

whether they are self-consistent or are self-refere ntially incoher-
ent, as Carl Henry puts it,[41] and how well they explain our
experience of reality.

I have suggested elsewhere an evangelical presuppositional
framework for biblical theology.[42] This is based on the notion that
God's truth, as it exists in the Bible, must be self-authenticating.
We can, therefore, examine the Scriptures to see if there is a
coherent and self-consistent understanding of truth and of how
we as thinking and rational beings can attain to it. The following,
I suggest, summarises the biblical position:

 i.   God, who made all things, exists and he alone, as the
      creator of all things, interprets the meaning of things
      and events.
 ii. Being created in the image of God, we know that we
      are dependent on God for the truth.
 iii. As sinners we suppress this knowledge and reinter-
      pret the universe on the basis that we give all things
      and events their meaning.
 iv. Special revelation, which not only informs us but is
      also redemptive, is needed to deal with our hostile
      suppression of the truth.
 v.   We will hear this redemptive word, the gospel of
      Christ, only as the Holy Spirit of God brings us to
      repentance and faith.

These presuppositions are arrived at by taking the Bible as
our source of information. They are part of our hermeneutical
spiral in which we move from assumption to text and back again
in order to develop an understanding of the reality presented in

---

[41] Carl F. H. Henry, *Toward a Recovery of Christian Belief* (Wheaton: Crossway
Books, 1990), 46. Henry refers to those presuppositions which cancel themselves
out. Thus, the empiricist makes the non-empirical assertion that only empirical
facts are true; the relativist uses an absolute statement to deny the possibility of
absolutes; the nihilist uses a meaningful proposition to assert that nothing has
meaning; the postmodern deconstructionist writes his intended meaning in a
text which denies that the author's intended meaning can ever be known or be
relevant.
[42] ' "Thus Says the Lord": The Dogmatic Basis of Biblical Theology.' P.T.
O'Brien & D.G. Peterson (eds), *God Who Is Rich in Mercy* (Homebush: Lancer,
1986), and in my *According to Plan* (Leicester: IVP, 1991), 54–56.

the Bible. The reason we have such presuppositions is that the message about Jesus Christ has arrested us and brought us to a new mind about God and his word. This must be our starting point for a biblical theology. The doubts that various scholars have expressed about the viability of biblical theology are essentially doubts about the viability of evangelical presuppositions. The exact nature of biblical theology is, of course, a matter for continuing debate.

Thus, it is the apostolic testimony to the gospel that must structure our understanding of the way God's revelation has come to us in the Bible. We are driven by the gospel to understand both the mode of revelation and the content of it. The introduction to the Epistle to the Hebrews points to the reality of the two testaments and to their unity: God spoke in former times through the prophets, and has spoken in these last days through his Son. The exposition of the OT in the light of Christ, which this epistle gives, shows up the historically structured unity and distinction that characterises the word of the prophets and the word of Jesus.

What, then, is the apostolic gospel which must govern our understanding of biblical theology? If we view the gospel as event, then it is the defining parameters of the event which mark out the content of the gospel. If we view the gospel as the proclamation of the event, the same parameters apply. Proclamation without the event is powerless to save, but the event needs to be proclaimed if people are to believe it (Rom 10:5–17). The four gospels agree that the parameters of the gospel are those of the earthly existence of Jesus of Nazareth culminating in his death on the cross, his resurrection and ascension to the Father in heaven. The gospel includes the God-given interpretation of the events of Jesus. Thus we must accept that this Jesus fulfils the promises of God; that he lived and died for the sake of others; that he was the God-man from heaven; that his life, death, and resurrection are the means and the grounds of our being put into right relationship with God.

The NT notion of the kingdom of God is the fulfilment of the OT. According to Mark, the gospel of God which Jesus preached contained certain basic elements (Mk 1:14,15). It was firstly a message of fulfilment. Both the literary and historical contexts of

the assertion that 'the time is fulfilled' would lead us to the
conclusion that Jesus understood the historically based prophetic
word of the OT to be at the point of fulfilment in his own ministry.
Secondly, the message concerned the arrival of the kingdom of
God. This can only mean that Jesus understood the content of the
prophetic message to be the coming of the kingdom of God. It is
clear from Luke 24:27,44,45 and other passages that Jesus
understood that the OT was about him and his saving ministry.

Not only was the resurrection and exaltation of Jesus the climax
of the gospel event, it was the reaching of the goal of the OT. An
analysis of the preaching of the gospel shows how this message
of Jesus was taken up in the post-Pentecost apostolic church.[43]

  i.   The note of fulfilment of the OT Scriptures was promi-
       nent.
  ii. The content of the message was the person of Jesus of
       Nazareth in his life, death, and resurrection.
  iii. The coming of the kingdom is a reality in the present
       rule of the ascended and exalted Christ.
  iv. The whole of the OT message reaches its goal in the
       resurrection and exaltation of Jesus.

Our basic premise is that all theologising should be controlled
by the gospel. From the summary above we conclude that the
apostles certainly regarded the message about Jesus as definitive
for all theologising. It is the message about the life, death, and
resurrection of Jesus to which the whole Bible, both Old and NTs,
testify. It is not that God could not, or did not, say anything apart
from Christ in the gospel, for we are told that the creation testifies
to his glory. But we must hasten to add that the creation revelation
and the gospel revelation, though distinct, are not to be separated.
After all, it is the gospel which is bringing the regeneration of the
whole cosmos. The ultimate meaning of the cosmos and its des-
tiny can only be found in the gospel. The gospel tells us that the
redemptive work of God is to be found in Christ alone. Redemptive history in the OT is therefore somehow about Christ. The

---

[43] This has been amply demonstrated in C. H. Dodd's classic treatment of the
apostolic gospel in *The Apostolic Preaching and its Developments* (London: Hodder
and Stoughton, 1944).

inescapable dimension in all this is the historical process which leads to the coming of the Word of God in the incarnation of Jesus.

The centrality of the gospel to the Bible and its theology is thus established by the NT. This has a number of ramifications for the way we do theology and the way we thus think about reality. It demands that our starting point is the self-authenticating word of God so that we develop a hermeneutics of revelation and grace, not of human autonomy and nature. Creation cannot be separated from redemption since the ultimate plan of God in creation is defined in terms of Christ (Col 1:15–17). Regeneration of the universe is not merely a rehabilitation job but rather the purpose for which generation (creation) was initially effected.

The gospel pattern of redemption is definitive for understanding all notions of redemption in the Bible. Thus, redemptive history in the OT, which is fulfilled in the gospel, takes its pattern from the gospel. This is not to say that there is not something self-evident about the structure of the OT which helps us in our interpretation of the NT. But, if the word of God in Jesus can be characterised as God's fullest revelation, then the principal focus must be on the interpretation of the OT by the gospel. Now, the climax of the gospel message is clearly the exaltation of the crucified Christ. How then does the OT present a foreshadowing of this event? If we were left to look for a murdered redeemer rising from the dead in the OT it would indeed be a puzzle. But the gospel is proclaimed by Jesus and the apostles in terms of OT events in a way which establishes the gospel as the hermeneutical key.

This is why I am firmly of the conviction that the three-fold structure taught to me by Donald Robinson is superior to, and more theologically productive than, the structures proposed by Vos, Clowney, and VanGemeren. Donald Robinson has pinpointed the gospel structure in the OT rather than merely a series of consecutive periods. These periods, of course, exist, but their interrelatedness and relation to the gospel is crucial to a viable and powerful biblical theology. The other writers mentioned do indeed recognise the goal of the whole of the OT in Christ. But it seems that they have tended to work more from a descriptive approach to the OT as it leads them to Christ. The gospel demands that we start with Jesus Christ and the apostolic gospel

to see how the OT is conceived as that which testifies to Christ
and shows God at work to redeem his people. The following
points may be made:

i. The gospel is understood in terms of OT redemptive history climaxing in David and Solomon

In the course of expounding the meaning of Jesus and his death
and resurrection, the NT writers focus on him and understand
him as creator, word of God, Adam, son of Abraham, Israel, son
of David, prophet, priest, king, wise man, temple and so on. The
very first Christian sermon identifies the resurrection with the
fulfilment of the rule of the Davidic king (Acts 2:30–36). There is
an historical and redemptive logic to all this which corresponds
to the structure of the OT. Creation and fall are the indispensable
precursors to redemptive history, which is why creation and
Eden are so closely linked to the later eschatology. In the meantime themes such as the promised land maintain the essential
link. Creation and fall, then, lead to the election of Israel and
redemption culminating in the Davidic kingdom with the temple at its centre. There is manifest diversity in the historical
process and an undeniable imperfection, but the pattern is nevertheless clear. The recreative-redemptive process in the history
of humankind is found exclusively in the biblical history which
focuses on the affairs of Israel and climaxes in the Davidic-
Solomonic rule in Jerusalem.

ii. The prophetic eschatology is a recapitulation of the history of redemption in Israel

The inbuilt ambiguity of the historical process in the OT, due to
the innate propensity of even the elect to rebel against grace,
does not leave us without help. The prophetic word provides a
recapitulation of the redemptive-history of Israel when it addresses the problem of sin and judgment. The history of Israel
shows a degeneration from the time of Solomon's apostasy. This
fact could be said to highlight the climax of redemptive history
in 1 Kings 1–10, for thereafter it is a slide into destruction. But
the prophetic word emphasises that alongside rebellion and
judgment there is the sovereign purpose of a gracious God.

Prophetic eschatology, then, projects the future, perfect, and glorious fulfilment of God's purposes for his people in a kingdom yet to come. This eschatology is set against the historical background of the destruction of Israel and Judah and the Babylonian exile. It could be argued that prophetic eschatology begins with the promises to David in 2 Samuel 7 and there is no reason why epochs of redemptive revelation should not overlap. The historic dynasty of David, and the idealised prophetic dynasty are thus linked. While the restoration of the exiles under Cyrus is seen as in some sense a fulfilment of the prophetic promises, it is incomplete and lacking in the perfection and glory which are integral to the promises. Thus the OT closes in tension between promise and the non-experience of fulfilment.

iii. The gospel shows the epochal structure of redemptive history from Abraham to Solomon

We must conclude, then, that a gospel-based approach to the structure of the OT leads us to recognise two primary epochs or expressions of the coming of the kingdom of God which foreshadow the gospel. Following the lead given by Donald Robinson we can state these as the kingdom revealed in the history of Israel from Abraham to Solomon, and secondly as the kingdom of God revealed in prophetic eschatology. The unity of these two expressions lies in the prophetic recapitulation of the historical events of election, exodus redemption from captivity, law, entry and possession of the land, Davidic kingship, temple and Jerusalem. The distinction lies in the prophetic understanding that the eschatological event will transcend the historical by being perfect, glorious, and eternal. The logic lies in the fact that the prophetic recapitulation is from creation to new creation, but that this cosmic regeneration is inseparable from the renewal of the redemptive events from the Abrahamic covenant to the high-point of David's kingship and Solomon's temple. And that is the emphasis found in the NT.

iv. The pivotal point of redemption is the resurrection

The heart of my argument, then, is this: *the pivotal point in redemption is the resurrection and exaltation of the Christ. The New*

Testament itself identifies this event as that which corresponds to the establishing of the Davidic rule and the temple. This in no way should be seen as depreciating the importance of the cross. The cross presupposes that the suffering servant-messiah will be vindicated.[44] The resurrection presupposes the death on the cross, so that it is the suffering servant-messiah who is raised and vindicated (justified).

v. The gospel shapes the NT view of how the kingdom of God comes with the tension of the 'now' and the 'not yet'

The NT proclaims that the kingdom of God foreshadowed in OT history and promised in prophecy has come in Jesus of Nazareth. He is the kingdom of God. Part of the tension in the NT is the perception that Jesus of Nazareth does not fulfil the expectations of the Jews which they saw as the implications of the OT promises. Even the disciples found it hard to grasp that the Christ should suffer and then enter into his glory (Luke 24:25–27). Once again it is the gospel which shapes the NT view of the coming of the kingdom. What is often spoken of as the tension between the 'now' and the 'not yet' is a function of the way God brings in his kingdom. Since the kingdom comes with Jesus, we see the coming of the kingdom in the coming of Jesus, and the manner of its coming depends on the manner of Jesus' coming. In his first coming he is revealed as the last Adam, the seed of Abraham, the faithful Israel, the son of David. In his resurrection he, as the covenant-keeper, is justified and accepted into the eternal presence of the Father. This representative and substitutionary role of Jesus only touches others if the kingdom somehow comes to them also. This happens with the coming of the exalted Christ in his word and by his Spirit. Those who are united to him by faith find that they now experience the

---

[44] We might note that Jesus' use of Psalm 22:1 is not an isolated verse as a cry of despair. He had declared that he had power both to lay down his life and to take it again (John 10:18). The psalmist expressed both suffering in the face of persecution and the confidence that he would be vindicated, for which he praises God. I suggest that Jesus maintained the confidence of eventual vindication even in the face of his suffering. Thus he can say to the thief, 'Today you will be with me in paradise'.

kingdom tension in themselves. They are in the kingdom in their representative, but in themselves they are strangers and pilgrims in the world. The resolution of the tension is promised in the return of Jesus in glory to consummate universally what is already a reality in him.

vi. Towards a definition of biblical theology

It can now be suggested that what we mean by biblical theology is the theology as it is presented in the Bible within the historical process of progressive revelation. It is structured by the way the biblical authors did theology, and in particular by the gospel as it is expounded in terms of Jesus of Nazareth being the goal and fulfilment of redemptive history in the OT. Biblical theology seeks to understand the 'big picture' of divine revelation. It is difficult to state a concise working definition which will find general acceptance.[45] Much depends on the stance taken and the assumptions made. In the light of our discussion we might propose the following: biblical theology is the study of the gospel in the context of its antecedents and its effects as these are set out in the whole canon of Scripture.

vii. The question of a centre or controlling theme in biblical theology

One final matter in the question of the viability of biblical theology needs to be mentioned. Much has been written about the attempts to identify a single unifying theme or centre for a biblical theology. The very endeavour, of course, assumes that there is some essential unity to the theology of the whole Bible. For an evangelical this means something like accepting that the Bible is the one word of the one God about the one way of salvation. But even some conservative writers who accept in

---

[45] Following the presentation of these papers at the School of Theology, these definitions were suggested by Richard Blight, a student at Moore College: i. Biblical theology is the study of the main theme or themes of the Bible and the way that they are presented and developed in the Scriptures. It then involves the study of how the various parts of the Bible relate to this theme or themes. ii. Biblical theology is the study of the theme or themes which establish the unity and coherence of the Bible. It also involves the study of how the various parts of the Bible relate to this theme or themes.

principle the unity of the Bible question the attempts to express
this unity in terms of one theme.

The kingdom of God as the organising principle

I have no doubt that my own attempt to identify a unifying
theme in the notion of the kingdom of God was largely influenced by John Bright's book of that name. Charles Scobie has
criticised my choice because the term primarily occurs in the
synoptic gospels and nowhere in the OT.[46] But it is difficult to
see the force of his objection, since he concedes that major themes
can be identified by a more general expression such as the 'rule
of God'. Mostly, the rejection of such an approach seems to
reflect a nervousness about imposing an artificial unity on the
Bible. But caution about artificial schemes should not divert us
from recognising the implications of both the canon and the
gospel for the unity of the Bible.

The need to distinguish terms, themes, and theological concepts

It appears that we need to differentiate between a word or
phrase (such as God, or kingdom of God), a theme (such as
temple, or redemption), and the theological principle which
might underlie such words or themes. In reply to Scobie, use of
kingdom of God is one of legitimate reductionism and theological abstraction, not an attempt to identify the synoptic use of the
term in every part of the Bible. Not only would I suggest that the
rule of God and the kingdom of God are equally useful for the
purpose, but that what we are looking for is the theological
underpinning for the entire biblical message, not merely a theme
that runs the length of the biblical story.

A multi-thematic approach is viable

Scobie seems to miss the point that, according to the synoptics,
Jesus begins his ministry (Mark 1:14,15) with a reference to the

---

[46] 'The Structure of Biblical Theology', *Tyndale Bulletin*, 42/1 (1991), 177.

kingdom of God as the fulfilment. Jesus implies that this has meaning for the Jews who are oriented to the OT scriptures. It is clearly not the term as such but the theological concept that Jesus refers to. Scobie proposes a multi-thematic approach to doing biblical theology. I have employed such an approach in *According to Plan*,[47] where alongside the theme of the kingdom of God is placed the theme of creation and new creation, and also the wisdom-oriented theme of order and regeneration of order.

A multi-thematic approach still needs a unifying principle

A multi-thematic approach only makes sense if there is some identifiable theological theme or concept which underlies all themes. If we cannot assume this we have no basis for asserting the theological unity of the Bible. It is at this level that the interaction of biblical and systematic theology is most fruitful. Thus when the term 'kingdom of God' is proposed as the theological centre of the Bible it is in a conceptual and reductionist way. The biblical literature, as literature, does not easily yield a centre. But the biblical revelation, as revelation, does provide us with a base to work from into every text of the Bible and towards a unified biblical theology. The reason it is not helpful to make 'God' the unifying principle is that it needs definition by the gospel and does not account for the biblical distinction between God and his creation. We need another more explicit base.

All themes lead to the gospel of the kingdom

This base is the gospel which is the message that the sovereign creator Lord God has made all things for himself and has acted in redemptive history, which centres in Jesus Christ's life, death, and resurrection, in order to restore all things to their appointed place under his rule. To those evangelical theologians who doubt the viability of such a unified biblical theology and who adopt the multiple theologies approach, as well as a multiple

---

[47] G. Goldsworthy, *According to Plan: The Unfolding Revelation of God in the Bible* (Leicester: IVP, 1991).

theme approach, I have but one question: if all these diverse theologies and themes do not point to and centre in the real Christ of all history, to the dying, rising and exalted Christ, where in heaven or earth do they point?

Exploring further

1. Some older biblical theologies were criticised for being merely a process of proof-texting existing dogmatics. Do you think biblical theology can, or even should, function in this way?
2. How would you defend a presuppositional approach to the authority and unity of the Bible? Should such a basic defence be taught to young Christians?
3. Consider the view that biblical theology is indispensable to the proper interpretation of the Bible.
4. How would you relate the predominant salvation-history in the Bible to the theology of creation and to the wisdom literature?
5. What kind of relationship exists between biblical theology and Christian doctrine?

Biblical Theology and Biblical Interpretation
Barry Webb

Synopsis

The first part of this paper argues that biblical theology is not an end in itself but the foundational element of the wider task of biblical interpretation. For evangelicals, biblical theology is the articulation of their gospel-based understanding of the nature of the text (the Bible) which they are reading. But the normative nature of this text necessarily entails moving beyond biblical theology itself to systematic theology and ethical reflection, without losing the gospel focus which biblical theology provides. The body of the paper then takes Mark 1:14,15 as the starting point for an exploration of the process of moving from the gospel to the formulation of an evangelical hermeneutic in this more comprehensive sense, and identifies some of the distinguishing features of the kind of hermeneutic which results. These include a commitment to the historical reference of the biblical text, its theological coherence, and the rule of God reflected in it. Repentance is identified as both starting point and goal of such a hermeneutic. The paper ends with reflections on the role of the Holy Spirit, Christian community, and dialogue with outsiders in the practice of an authentically evangelical hermeneutic.

So far in this volume the focus has been on biblical theology itself. Now it is time to consider its relationship to a range of other things, beginning in this paper with an evangelical approach to interpreting Scripture. I will come to the distinctives

of evangelicalism in due course, but begin with some more
general observations.

Preliminary comments on biblical hermeneutics in general

Fundamental to all responsible use of the Bible is what I will refer
to here as the art of biblical hermeneutics. By hermeneutics I
mean the process of reading a text with a view to understanding
what it is about. Most texts, of course, are about many things,
either simultaneously or in succession. But I take it that understanding at the most fundamental level can arise only by considering how the particulars of the text interact with one another
and what 'meaning effect' results from this interaction. Any
attempt to state what the text is about in this sense will need to
do justice not just to the particulars themselves, but the complex
relationships between them. It is obvious from the outset that
this is a daunting task, and that any claim to have understood
the text in this way must be provisional and open to correction
by interpretations which commend themselves as more
adequate. Hermeneutics is a never-ending process.

By 'biblical' hermeneutics I mean hermeneutics which has the
Bible as its object. I do not mean to imply that there is no such
thing as biblical hermeneutics in the normative sense (hermeneutics which conforms in its basic principles to biblical teaching). Indeed I will end up commending an approach to
hermeneutics which I believe is in fact biblical in this sense. But
that is not the sense in which I am using the term at this point.
When I do use it in the normative sense I trust that the shift will
be sufficiently clear from the context that no confusion will arise.
Nor is the holistic sense in which I am talking about biblical
hermeneutics meant to deny the validity of focussing for particular purposes on relatively small parts of the Bible, even single
verses. But if what I have said so far is accepted, no adequate
statement of the meaning of such small units can be made
without some reference to their place in the Bible as a whole.[1]

---

[1] Cf D. A. Carson, *The Gagging of God. Christianity Confronts Pluralism* (Grand
Rapids: Zondervan, 1996), 131: '. . . recognition of the canon implicitly forbids
an atomistic approach to texts within the canon'.

## Biblical Theology and Biblical Interpretation 49

The parts cannot be understood without reference to the whole, and vice versa.

Finally, I have chosen the expression 'the *art* of biblical hermeneutics' advisedly. It has always seemed obvious to me that biblical hermeneutics as a discipline belongs fundamentally to the domain of the arts and humanities rather than the sciences. The distinction is perhaps best illustrated by considering the differing ways in which human beings are studied in the typical university context. The sciences characteristically concentrate on their physiology and biology and their development as a species in so far as it can be reconstructed from material remains. The humanities typically focus on them as volitional beings who express their personalities through creative activities such as speech, literature, art, and various kinds of social activity. Of course no absolute separation between art and science is either possible or desirable. Disciplines such as psychology and anthropology are related to the humanities by their subject matter and to the sciences by their methods. But the mere fact that we can speak this way confirms that the basic distinction is well recognised, and it is relevant to the issue at hand. The Bible is essentially a literary work, and reading it is much more like dialoguing with a person than dissecting a body.[2] Admittedly biblical hermeneutics depends in various ways on co-lateral disciplines such as linguistics and archaeology, which belong quite clearly to the human sciences rather than to the humanities as such. It also has rational thought, including the critical evaluation arguments, in common with these other disciplines. But what I want to maintain here is that such disciplines should not be confused with biblical hermeneutics itself.

Biblical hermeneutics as interpretation of the Bible presupposes agreement about what the Bible is (its canon and text), so that discussions in these areas belong logically to the category of prolegomena. The canon can reasonably be regarded as a given, at least for interpreters such as evangelicals, who belong to a more or less specific Christian tradition. Textual questions are far more complex and are not amenable to prior

[2] Cf M. Barth, *Conversation with the Bible* (New York: Holt, Rinehart and Winston, 1964).

settlement in such a global fashion. Hence interpreters will need to digress from the hermeneutical task itself at certain points to justify the text they are using. Other digressions will sometimes be needed to investigate the semantic range of a word or expression in a particular period, or to clarify historical reference in the text. But such digressions should be recognised for what they are. They will normally take interpreters into fields of background study of a more or less scientific kind, enabling them to draw upon the work of specialists in these areas. But for biblical hermeneutics the primary focus is on the Bible itself, and how its parts interact with one another to convey its message or messages. It is not the particular task of biblical hermeneutics to re-invent the Bible, or to use it as a source for studying something else (eg the history of Israel), but to read it with a view to understanding it as it stands, in the main employing skills which belong properly to the field of literary appreciation, and therefore fundamentally to the arts.[3]

This is a contentious point, and it is certainly not the whole truth about hermeneutics. I myself will qualify it in a number of important ways in what follows. But if it can be accepted provisionally at this point it will serve two very valuable purposes. It will focus us on the Bible itself as a given reality: its structure, literary character, its diversity and coherence. Second, it will make us more sensitive than we might otherwise be to the interplay of the objective and the subjective in the reading process. These are the most fundamental issues in the art of biblical hermeneutics: the nature of the Bible, the nature of the reader, and what happens when the two are brought together in the reading process.

We are now in a position to approach the central concern of this paper more directly by asking the question. What will be the

---

[3] Note the plethora of works in recent years concerning the 'artfulness' of biblical texts and their interpretation, eg R. Alter, *The Art of Biblical Narrative* (New York: Basic Books, 1981); *The Art of Biblical Poetry* (New York: Basic, 1985); J. P. Long, *The Art of Biblical History* (Grand Rapids: Zondervan, 1994), and the many literary studies and guides.

effect on the reading process if the reader is an evangelical? What special characteristics will the activity of interpretation assume in this case? Or to put it another way, what is the distinctive nature of evangelical hermeneutics?

Defining evangelical hermeneutics

It would be possible to speak of evangelical hermeneutics in a purely descriptive sense by surveying the range of interpretive methods which evangelicals either use, or have used, and trying to distil out of them some common or core characteristics. This would no doubt be an interesting and valuable exercise, but it is not what I am about here. Instead I want to raise a far more fundamental issue. Given that an evangelical, by definition, is a person profoundly influenced by and committed to the evangel, what kind of hermeneutic should follow? In other words, what kind of hermeneutic is implied by the gospel itself?

Evangelicals, the gospel and pre-understanding

Since the work of Gadamer in the 1960s, discussion of hermeneutics has largely been concerned with the role that pre-understanding plays in the interpretive process.[4] As they approach the text, readers' minds are not blank receptors, ready to absorb passively whatever the text delivers. On the contrary, readers bring a state of mind and a way of seeing the world (including the text) which has been developed by the whole complex of experiences that has made them what they are, and the interpretive process which they then embark upon consists of a merging of their own horizon (or world view) with that of the text.

Now evangelicals are clearly people for whom this process is already well advanced. The gospel which has so powerfully impacted upon them has come to them, directly or indirectly,

---

[4] H. G. Gadamer, *Truth and Method* (tr and rev by J. Weinsheimer & D. G. Marshall; New York: Crossroad, 1991 [1960]). For a concise but helpful discussion see Carson, *The Gagging of God*, 68–70.

from the Bible, and their understanding of what the Bible itself
is has been significantly shaped, in turn, by that gospel.[5] Evangelicals do not all express the gospel in the same way, but they
certainly share a great deal of common ground on what its basic
elements are. And they would agree that the most powerful
influence in shaping their common understanding has been the
way the gospel is articulated in the preaching and teaching of
Christ and his apostles in the NT. But it takes only a few minutes
reflection on the classic NT formulations of the gospel[6] to realise
that they have profound implications for an evangelical (gospel-
based) understanding of the nature of the Bible as a whole,
especially its theological coherence. Unfortunately, there is far
less agreement among evangelicals about the nature of the Bible
than about the gospel.[7] Discussion in this area has largely centred around questions such as inerrancy which have arisen more
as a response to modernism than out of reflection on the nature
of the gospel. The result is that interpretation of Scripture by
evangelicals has lacked the kind of controls necessary to give it
a clear gospel focus.

The crucial role of biblical theology

Graeme Goldsworthy's paper on the viability of biblical theology is an example of reflection on the nature of the gospel
leading to the articulation of an understanding of the nature of
the Bible as a whole. All evangelicals have a biblical theology,
however primitive. In this sense it is a given, and effectively the
pre-understanding which shapes their hermeneutics. But the
elaboration of it is a major part of the interpretive process itself.

---

[5] Cf T. G. Long, *Preaching and the Literary Forms of the Bible* (Philadelphia:
Fortress, 1989), 29: '. . . encounters with Scripture itself have built up in the
community of faith the expectation of Scripture's special character, rather than
the other way round. The expectations a faithful interpreter brings to Scripture
are not imposed on those documents entirely from without but are derived from
the history of the community's previous engagement with the Bible'.

[6] Eg Mark 1:8, Acts 2:22–36, or Romans 1:1–6.

[7] As an illustration see the published debate in articles and letters between Dunn
and Nicole in *The Churchman*: J. D. G. Dunn, 'The Authority of Scripture According to Scripture', *Churchman* 96 (1982), 104–122, 201–225; R. Nicole, 'The Inspiration and Authority of Scripture: J. D. G. Dunn versus B. B. Warfield, *Churchman*
97 (1983), 198–215; (1984), 198–216.

It is not my intention here to repeat what Graeme has said, or to offer either a defence or critique of it, except to say that I am in fundamental agreement with his conclusions. Biblical theology of this kind is unlikely ever to command universal consent, even among those who share its basic understanding of the gospel, and it certainly doesn't answer all the questions we rightly have about the nature of Scripture. But it is definitely evangelical in the principled way in which I have used that term above. Graeme has shown us how reflection on the nature of the NT gospel has profoundly shaped his own understanding of the character of the Bible as whole, especially the relationship between the testaments, and its fundamental theological coherence. The question is: If a biblical theology of a more or less Robinson-Goldsworthy kind is adopted, what will follow from it?

Biblical theology and evangelical hermeneutics

Here we have reached a most interesting point in our discussion. The general intent of my argument so far has been to emphasise the foundational importance of biblical theology. But have I perhaps unwittingly assigned it too limited a role? Could it be that it is not only a fundamental component of evangelical hermeneutics, but the sum total of it? Is biblical theology perhaps the only kind of hermeneutics evangelicals need?

It is not hard to establish at least a prima facie case that this is in fact so. I began this paper by defining biblical hermeneutics as the process of reading the Bible in order to understand what it is about at the most fundamental level. Now biblical theology seems to have provided us with a way of doing just that; potentially at least, it enables us to see every part of the Bible in relation to the gospel which lies at its heart. And since it is precisely to the ministry of that gospel that we are called as evangelicals, what more hermeneutics do we need before proceeding directly to preaching, teaching and so on? We may need to go on refining our biblical theology, but should we not see biblical theology more as the pre-understanding we need for Christian living and ministry rather than for further hermeneutics, especially if that hermeneutics is different in some way from biblical theology itself?

The fact of the matter, however, is that evangelicals have always found it necessary to engage in other kinds of hermeneutics, and it would be naïve to think that a recognition of the importance of biblical theology would change this. Furthermore, an expectation that it should do so could arise only from a false view of the nature of biblical theology itself. Evangelicals rightly hold to the normativeness of Scripture as the ultimate standard by which all claims about what Christians ought to believe or do must be evaluated. But it is this very normativeness of Scripture that necessitates other ways of studying the Bible than belong properly to the field of biblical theology. So far as its distinctive method is concerned, biblical theology is descriptive. Its brief is to describe, as accurately as possible, the given canonical shape of the Bible's theology, or, to put it another way, the manner in which the biblical writers, in interaction with one another, develop and express their own theological concerns. But the ongoing normativeness of Scripture in a changing world means that we inevitably have to do more than this. Our own horizon contains many issues and urgent questions which cannot be addressed by simply describing what the biblical writers said to their contemporaries. We have to formulate doctrines and establish guidelines for Christian conduct which use the materials of Scripture but configure them in new ways. In short, unless we are content with a purely antiquarian interest in Scripture, we need Bible-based systematic theology and ethics as well as biblical theology itself. The commitment of evangelicals to the normativeness of Scripture means that they must have a hermeneutic which is bigger than biblical theology, though it may rest on biblical theology as its foundation.

The relationship between biblical theology and ethics is the subject of a separate paper in this volume, so I will not dwell on it here. Suffice it to say that, in so far that it is based on an understanding of Scripture which is shaped by the gospel, it should be regarded as an aspect of evangelical hermeneutics.[8]

---

[8] For a good example see O. O'Donovan, *Resurrection and Moral Order* (Leicester: IVP/Apollos, 2nd ed, 1994).

The relationship between biblical theology and systematics will be reflected on further below. But if I am right in holding that Bible-based systematics is a necessary element of evangelical hermeneutics, it follows that historical theology, in as much as it concerns itself with the historical development of evangelical systematics, is also an indispensable part of evangelical hermeneutics. This historical awareness is important for sensitising us to the fact that evangelical hermeneutics is never simply a matter of personal, contemporary encounter with the Bible. Evangelicals, no less than others, read the Bible as members of an interpretive community with a history, and an awareness of that history should enable us to have a more sober and critical perception of our own contemporary encounter with Scripture than might otherwise be the case. Engagement with the history of evangelical hermeneutics, in even a preliminary way, would carry us far beyond the specific terms of reference of this paper. I simply wish to signal the importance of the topic, and to register my gratitude to Bishop Robinson for the contribution he has already made to alerting us to some of the factors which have shaped the biblical theology, and therefore the kind of evangelical hermeneutics, espoused by this college.

The essential characteristics of evangelical hermeneutics

Given that evangelical hermeneutics is bigger than biblical theology, what are its essential characteristics? For good and obvious reasons, what follows will overlap with earlier papers to some extent. Because of the crucial role of biblical theology in the interpretive process, we will have to revisit it from time to time in considering evangelical hermeneutics more generally. Even when we are not talking about it directly, it will be implicit in everything we do. But what I am trying to identify here are the essential characteristics of evangelical hermeneutics as a whole, from exegesis, through biblical theology, to systematic theology and ethical reflection.

With this in mind we will take the summary of Jesus' gospel proclamation in Mark 1:14,15 as a basic hermeneutic key. This will no doubt appear arbitrary and reductionistic to some, so, before proceeding, we must pause to consider the grounds on which such an approach may be justified.

Mark 1:14,15 as a hermeneutic key

The first justification is that I am not attempting here to develop a complete theoretical framework for evangelical hermeneutics, but to illustrate the kind of reasoning which is basic to such an enterprise, and to show some of the essential characteristics of the kind of hermeneutic that would result. For this purpose the selection of one classic formulation of the gospel is entirely appropriate.

The second justification is the purely pragmatic one that in a paper of this size, if we are ever to get past talking about what the gospel is, a selection of some kind is unavoidable. The gospel is formulated in different ways as we move from one part of the NT to another: from the synoptics to the fourth gospel, from the gospels in general to Acts, and from Acts to the epistles. There are also variations of perspective as we move from one biblical writer to another: Matthew to Mark, Mark to Luke, Luke to Paul, Paul to Peter, Peter to John, and so on. I would maintain that all these formulations are complementary rather than contradictory, but that is too big an issue to deal with here.[9]

Third, among the various NT formulations of the gospel, those which the biblical writers attribute directly to Jesus himself may rightly be considered foundational to all the others. After all, it was Jesus who commissioned the apostles and not vice versa.[10]

---

[9] As an example of such complementarity, compare the realised eschatology of John (salvation/eternal life as a present possession) with the final eschatology of Hebrews or 1 Peter (salvation as a future attainment). These may quite justifiably be seen as aspects of a larger truth (inaugurated eschatology) which recognises that salvation begins in the present and is consummated in the future. Cf G. R. Osborne, *The Hermeneutical Spiral. A Comprehensive Introduction to Biblical Interpretation* (Downers Grove: IVP, 1991), 268.

[10] I do not mean to imply that all the New Testament writers are apostles, but the majority were, and those who were not apostles themselves (eg Mark, Luke) were closely associated with them.

Furthermore, the issue of canonical arrangement is relevant here. The four gospels, which give direct eyewitness accounts of Jesus' ministry, occupy a position in the NT analogous to that of the Torah in the Old. As the rest of the OT is in a very real sense exposition of the Torah, so the rest of the New is exposition of the gospels. So if our object is to find a classic foundational formulation of the NT gospel, it is to the gospels we should look, and to Jesus in particular as the gospels bear witness to him.

Finally, the key elements of the way the gospel is presented in Mark 1:15 (the concepts of a particularly significant 'time', fulfilment, the kingdom of God, and the need to repent and believe) are all widely represented in the way the gospels generally present the ministry of Jesus.[11] The fourth gospel is distinctive in certain respects, but even here the links with the same basic concepts are strong. The ideas of a 'time' and of fulfilment are both present, the latter especially so.[12] The concept of the kingdom of God is brought into direct contact with the Johannine themes of the new birth and eternal life in chapter 3, and the issue of Jesus' kingship and the nature of his kingdom features centrally in the account of his trial and passion.[13] In contrast to the synoptics, there is no explicit demand for repentance in John's gospel. Instead the accent falls on 'believing'.[14] But Mark 1:15 combines the respective emphases of the synoptics and the fourth gospel with its twofold call: 'repent, and believe'.

In short, the choice made is not arbitrary. If it is granted that the Bible has a basic storyline, the announcement in Mark 1:14,15 comes, on any reckoning, at a critical point.[15] It can reasonably

---

[11] Eg a significant time: Matt 13:30; 26:18; Mark 13:33; Luke 12:56; 19:44; 21:8; John 7:6,8. Fulfilment: Matt 4:14; 26:54; 26:56; Mark 14:49; Luke 4:21; 22:16; 22:37; 22:44. Kingdom of God/heaven: Matt 4:17; 4:23; 5:3, etc; Luke 4:43; 9:60; 10:9; John 3:3,5. Repent, believe: Matt 4:17; 11:20; 21:32; Mark 6:12; Luke 13:3,5; John 1:50; 3:12,16,18; 4:21,42,48; 5:38,44,46, etc.

[12] Significant time: 7:6,8. Fulfilment: 12:38; 13:18; 17:12,13; 19:36.

[13] See 18:33,36,37,39; 19:3,12,14,15,19,21, and cf 1:49; 12:13,15.

[14] Believing is mentioned in 50 verses in all.

[15] I am taking the gospels as a whole as joint witnesses to the same crucial event, or cluster of events: the advent of the Messiah, and especially his public ministry. If any justification is needed for choosing Mark 1:14,15 over, say, Matthew 4:17, its more comprehensive character and the almost universal scholarly acknowledgment of Marcan priority should be sufficient.

be seen as a summary of the earwitness testimony to the terms in which Jesus characteristically proclaimed the gospel. As such it is foundational to all other formulations of the gospel in the NT. If space permitted we could map the echoes of it in the apostolic preaching of Acts, and in the epistles, but that must be left to another occasion.[16] We have laid sufficient foundations to proceed with the main line of our inquiry, namely, what would be the character of an evangelical hermeneutic which is shaped in all its parts by the gospel summary of Mark 1:14,15? Evangelical hermeneutics in general will undoubtedly have more dimensions to it than this limited exercise will bring to light, but we should at least be able to identify its essential features.

Towards an evangelical hermeneutic
The passage we have chosen reads as follows:

> [14]Now after John was arrested, Jesus came into Galilee, preaching the gospel of God [15]and saying, "The time is fulfilled, and the kingdom of God is at hand; repent, and believe in the gospel".

We will focus primarily on the gospel proclamation itself in verse 15, but with careful attention also to the way this is nuanced by the introduction provided by verse 14.

Evangelical hermeneutics and history
Jesus' preaching of the gospel is first of all an announcement that a particularly significant time has arrived, the time when the shell of expectation is filled up (fulfilled) with historical content. Furthermore, in view of the bracketing references to God, the

---

[16] For a start, one could note the close parallel between the content and structure of Mark's gospel and the preaching of Peter (eg Acts 10:34–43), the way Paul's gospel ministry can be summarised in terms of preaching the kingdom of God (Acts 20:25; 28:31; cf Rom 14:16), and the concept of the 'time fully come' in Christ in Pauline theology (Gal 4:4; Eph 1:10; cf 1 Cor 1:20). For further treatment see C. H. Dodd, *The Apostolic Preaching and its Developments* (London: Hodder and Stoughton, [1936]1944), 36–56, and *Move in for Action* (Report of the Commission on Evangelism of the Church of England, Diocese of Sydney; Sydney: Anzea, 1971), 49–73.

passive form of the verb 'is fulfilled' (*peplērōtai*) points to God himself as the filler.[17] And as the introduction in verse 14 makes clear, this announcement itself is made at a particular time ('after John was arrested') and in a particular place ('Galilee'). In other words, this classic formulation of the gospel establishes the strongest possible nexus between theology and history. It is interesting in this regard that Guelich in his Word commentary takes the expression 'the kingdom of God is at hand' in verse 15 to mean 'the kingdom has come into history'.[18] This has a number of important consequences for any hermeneutic which claims to be evangelical in the principled sense, especially at the level of exegesis and biblical theology. But before spelling them out we must note carefully a significant aspect of the way Mark uses the word 'gospel'.

In verse 15 it refers to an oral announcement. But in 1:1 ('The beginning of the gospel of Jesus Christ, the Son of God') it appears to refer generally to the content of the entire literary work which follows. In other words, Mark himself establishes the important link between gospel as oral proclamation and gospel as written text. Underlying the difference of genre there is a fundamental continuity of character. The written gospel is simply a fuller presentation of the oral gospel which is summarised in 1:14,15.[19] I will argue below that the same fundamental continuity exits between the preached gospel and Scripture as a whole, but for the moment it is sufficient to note the appropriateness of deriving principles from a summary of the preached gospel and applying them to the reading of biblical texts. What then are the implications for evangelical hermeneutics of this first basic characteristic of the gospel?

First, and most fundamentally, an evangelical hermeneutic will resist any attempt to break the nexus between the literary

---

[17] R. A. Guelich, *Mark 1–8:26* (WBC; Dallas: Word, 1989), 43.
[18] Guelich, 43.
[19] Guelich, 41, 42 classifies Mark 1:14–15 form critically as a 'summary report', and refers to others such as Mussner and Pesch who classify it more specifically within the genre of a prophetic summons as an 'opening statement'. 'The account of Jesus' ministry that follows (1:16–16:8) is synonymous with Jesus' preaching as expressed in 1:14,15. His work and words in 1:16–16:8 declare the coming of the appointed time and proclaim the kingdom of God.'

meaning of a biblical text and its historical reference. This is not
to retreat in the least from my earlier assertion that biblical
hermeneutics is an essentially literary discipline. As the gospel
is an announcement to be listened to ('He who has ears to hear,
let him hear', Matt 11:15), so the Bible is a text to be read ('Let
the reader understand', Matt 24:15). The fundamental task of
evangelical interpreters of Scripture is to be attentive readers,
with their primary focus on the text in its final, canonical form.
But they will recognise that, as the gospel is an announcement
made at a particular time and place, so the text came into being
in a particular period and situation, and that, to be true to the
text, their reading must necessarily take account of that fact.

This is the rationale for a principled rather than merely pragmatic engagement in biblical criticism by evangelicals. It stems
from a recognition of the human, historically connected nature
of Scripture, and biblical criticism, rightly understood, is an
exploration of the humanity of the text. An approach to biblical
studies which eschews biblical criticism in the name of divine
inspiration is essentially docetic, and not true to the character of
Scripture. Principled evangelicals will acknowledge that the
biblical text they are reading has a history, that its language is
historically conditioned, that meaning is to some extent genre
specific, and that in most cases the people, places and events
named in the text have a more complex existence outside it. They
will therefore welcome insights from historical study which
assist them to be judicious, responsible readers. They will refuse
to disconnect the text from history. But at the same time they will
recognise that, while word and event are closely bound together
in divine revelation, the word is primary. The gospel is an
announcement, a word, and therefore it is the word which
interprets events, not vice versa. The interpreter guided by the
gospel will value historical criticism as an ancillary discipline (or
field of disciplines) without allowing it to become the controlling
foundation on which hermeneutics rests.

A second implication relates particularly to the movement
from biblical theology to systematic theology, and to Christology in particular. The principled evangelical will resist the tendency to divorce theology from history by driving a wedge
between the 'Jesus of history' and the 'Christ of faith'. This

separation can come about in a number of different ways, of which we can mention only two here. First, it can happen through the very reversal between word and event that we have just been considering. The primary focus shifts from word to event, from text to background; the real Jesus is distinguished from the Jesus of biblical witness, and this 'real' Jesus becomes whatever historical study (sometimes of the most dubious kind) finds him to be.[20]

But the same thing can happen indirectly by falsely separating the epistles from the gospels, so that each is read without sufficient reference to the other, and two Christs are found within Scripture itself. This arises partly from a failure to recognise, or accept, that the nexus between the gospel and history forged in the preaching of Jesus himself is normative for the NT gospel as a whole. It stems also from a revisionist understanding of the resurrection which robs it of the historicity to which the apostolic preaching of Acts bears such unambiguous witness.[21] The effect is to disconnect Christology from its historical foundation in the gospel and turn it into a mere specialisation within the psychology of religion.

I have used Christology as an example because of its critical role in dogmatics and systematic theology. Failure to be guided by the gospel here, with its insistence on the fundamental connection between theology and history, will grossly distort the whole hermeneutical endeavour, especially at the business end where it impacts directly on the formulation of Christian doctrine.[22] The implications for ethics are equally serious, but I will leave that for Michael Hill to deal with in his paper.

This connection between theology and history is fundamental to evangelical hermeneutics because it is grounded in the

[20] Contrast B. Thiering, *Jesus the Man. A New Interpretation from the Dead Sea Scrolls* (New York: Doubleday, 1992), with N. T. Wright, *Who was Jesus?* (London: SPCK, 1992).

[21] Cf J. S. Spong, *Resurrection and Reality? A Bishop's Search for the Origins of Christianity* (San Francisco: Harper and Row, 1994), with P. Barnett, P. F. Jensen and D. G. Peterson, *Resurrection – Truth and Reality* (South Sydney: Aquila, 1994).

[22] For a review of the flight from history in New Testament studies and its effects on Christology see A. C. Thiselton, 'New Testament Interpretation in Historical Perspective', *Hearing the New Testament. Strategies for Interpretation* (ed J. B. Green; Grand Rapids: Eerdmans, 1995), 20–24.

nature of the gospel itself. It is part of the pre-understanding evangelicals bring to the interpretive task because they have already been impacted by that gospel and convinced of its truth. Evangelical hermeneutics cannot proceed with integrity without this being made clear from the start. This does not mean that the evangelical can or should opt out of the necessary and important business of defending the historical claims of the gospel, using whatever kinds of argument – historical, philosophical, and so on – that are appropriate to that task. It is simply to say that hermeneutics, and evangelical hermeneutics in particular, needs to be recognised as a distinct discipline with its own clearly identified starting point and rationale if it is to be saved from being endlessly sidetracked. We should not be surprised if, in the end, what is done in this way feeds back positively into apologetics. For if it is found that evangelicals are able to articulate a coherent theology and speak significantly to complex doctrinal and ethical issues on the basis of it, some at least of those who do not presently share our starting point may be provoked to considering its truth claims more closely. Evangelical apologetics and evangelical hermeneutics each have their own distinct brief. They are not the same, but they can and should be allies.

Evangelical hermeneutics and the theological coherence of the Bible

I have already commented briefly on the fact that the gospel summary of Mark 1:14,15 features fulfilment as a central element. We must now take this further and consider some of its implications for a gospel-based hermeneutic.

Guelich has pointed out that Mark 1:14,15 is not only programmatic for all that follows, but is also the concluding element of the preface which begins in 1:1.[23] The 'beginning of the gospel of Jesus Christ the Son of God' (1:1) reaches its climax in the gospel summary of 1:15. This makes the leading reference to 'Isaiah the prophet' in verse 2 an important key to understanding the idea of fulfilment in the preface as a whole. The

---

[23] Guelich, 41,42. The term 'programmatic' is my own; Guelich himself characterises 1:14,15 as a 'summary report'.

Isaianic prophecy of a voice crying in the wilderness, 'Prepare the way of the Lord' (1:2), is fulfilled in the ministry of John the baptiser (1:4–11). The reference to the arrest of John in 1:14 moves us beyond this to a further stage of fulfilment, but the sensitive reader cannot fail to see that this, too, moves against the backdrop of the book of Isaiah. It was Isaiah who prepared the word 'gospel' (*evangelion*) for its use here by filling it with rich theological content (Isa 40:9).[24] It was he who singled out Galilee as a place of key theological significance (Isa 9:2), and who summarised his own gospel in kingdom terms as 'Your God reigns' (Isa 52:7). In short, Jesus' gospel cannot be understood properly without recognising its intimate connection with Isaiah's gospel. The one is the fulfilment of the other.

What we see here is but a particular instance of a hermeneutical principle which pervades the entire NT. Mark's gospel itself sees the arrest of Jesus at the appropriate time as the fulfilment, not of this or that particular OT prophecy, but of 'the scriptures' in general (14:49). In the book of Acts the preaching of the gospel, especially to audiences familiar with the OT, characteristically takes the form of a review of the whole sweep of the divinely directed history of Israel, showing how it leads to the life, death and resurrection of Jesus the Messiah as its *telos* (Acts 13:16–39; cf. 2:22–53).[25] And the situation is fundamentally the same in the epistles. The NT as a whole contains at least 250 quotations from and 1100 allusions to the OT, showing that its theology rests on very broad OT foundations.[26] In other words, there is a fundamental theological coherence to the Bible implied by the gospel itself and reflected in the relationship between the two testaments. The implications for evangelical hermeneutics relate particularly to biblical theology, but have flow-on effects to other levels as well.

The specific task of biblical theology is to explore and describe this coherence as fully as possible. It is a complex, not

---

[24] Isaiah's *mebasseret* (herald) came across into the LXX as *evangelizomenos*", with a consequent impact on the NT *evangelion*.

[25] For a comparison of the Acts speeches with this point in mind, see *Move in for Action*.

[26] These figures are given by Osborne in *The Hermeneutical Spiral*, 277, citing the Nestle-Aland Greek New Testament.

simple coherence, so the task is no easy one, and biblical
theology constantly runs the danger of distorting the biblical
data by forcing it into a mould too rigid to contain it. Indeed,
given the diversity of authorship, genre, and theological traditions in Scripture, many doubt that biblical theology can be
done at all. But this is a counsel of despair not warranted by
the gospel. At the very least we can say that the promise-
fulfilment coherence between the testaments manifests itself in
the Bible as a whole in the form of an underlying storyline
running from creation and fall, through the call of Abraham
and the raising up of David, to the advent of Jesus the Messiah,
son of David, son of Abraham (Matt 1:1), and climaxing in a
new creation. So far attempts to refine this have taken a somewhat different character in Old and NT studies respectively. In
OT attention has been focused mainly on mapping the connections between the divergent theological traditions – law,
prophecy, wisdom, and apocalyptic – and the basic salvation
history storyline.[27] In NT most effort has centred around the
use of the OT in the New, and study of the individual corpora
– Lukan, Pauline, Johannine and so on – in order to identify
their distinctive emphases and the links between them. At the
macro level the quest has been for the single, unifying theme
of Scripture as a whole (eg promise, covenant, kingdom, hope,
presence, or communion) without any consensus emerging to
date.[28]

It is not my intention here to try to arbitrate between the
various approaches, but to make three points which are fundamental to the whole enterprise. First, the theological coherence
of Scripture is an implication of the gospel itself, so biblical
theology is possible. Second, progress is more likely if Old and
NT scholars work together than if they work independently. The

---

[27] Eg W. C. Kaiser, Jr, 'Wisdom Theology and the Centre of Old Testament
Theology', *EvQ* (July–Sept 1978), 132–46.

[28] For a good review of the issues, essentially from the perspective of a New
Testament scholar, see Osborne, *The Hermeneutical Spiral*, ch 13. Osborne con-
cludes, 'it is safe to say that most recognise that the Bible is too diverse in its
interests and emphases to be summed up in a single theme'. Cf D. A. Carson,
'Current Issues in Biblical Theology: A New Testament Perspective', *BBR* 5
(1995), 17–41.

task requires us to become students of the whole Bible. Biblical theology has to some extent been the victim of a theologically unjustified separation between Old and NT studies. And finally, the gospel commits us as evangelicals to the view that Jesus Christ himself is the unifying centre of biblical theology, however that is best expressed. What are the implications of this for systematic theology and ethical reflection?

First, a sound foundation of biblical theology will save systematics from the tendency to drift into proof-texting, by which I mean the formulation of doctrine using data drawn from Scripture without reference to the promise-fulfilment shape of the Bible's own theology. Texts used in formulating a doctrine of revelation, for example, will first be related to the Bible's basic plot line as contributing elements to what the Bible says about God and the salvation he has achieved in Christ. The individual biblical traditions and corpora will each be allowed to shed their own light on a topic before material is taken from them and combined into a more comprehensive framework. In other words, while there is a necessary systematising at this stage of hermeneutics which goes beyond that which the Bible itself engages in, this system will emerge, as far as possible, from the text via biblical theology, and this will mean that Scripture's own central focus on Christ and the gospel will not be lost.

Second, biblical theology has a critical role to play in the use of the OT in particular in ethical reflection. In dealing with a complex ethical issue such as homosexuality, for example, where the material that addresses it most explicitly is in the law of Moses, sound biblical theology will prevent the interpreter from either dismissing this material as fundamentally irrelevant, or of invoking it as directly prescribing Christian behaviour. Rather, it will raise larger issues about the relationship of the law to its fulfilment in Christ, and set the relevant ethical issues in the light of the gospel. For an example see my own paper on homosexuality in an earlier volume in this series.[29] At the level of social ethics, biblical theology will guard against the kind of

---

[29] B. G. Webb, 'Homosexuality in Scripture', *Explorations 8. Theological and Pastoral Responses to Homosexuality* (ed B. G. Webb; Adelaide: Openbook, 1994), 65–104.

reconstructionism which seeks to derive Christian economics and social policy directly from the OT, again without sufficient regard for the differences that the gospel brings.[30]

Evangelical hermeneutics and the rule of God

The gospel summary of Mark 1:15 contains two great affirmations which are structurally parallel to one another: 'the time is fulfilled', and 'the kingdom of God is at hand'. We have looked at the first; now it is time to give our attention to the second. Since the two are parallel they cannot be properly understood in isolation from one another. The second expresses fundamentally the same truth as the first: the time that has been fulfilled is the time for the kingdom of God to be at hand in the life and ministry of Jesus. But there is an additional nuance which relates particularly to the expression 'the kingdom of God'.

This is primarily a salvation-history concept, and the implications for biblical theology of its central place in the preaching of Jesus are huge. However, since these have been dealt with in the previous two papers, we need not dwell on them here. Suffice it to say that I am assuming an ontological connection between the preached gospel as summarised here and Scripture as a whole. If anything is needed to substantiate this beyond what has already been said in this and earlier papers, I would simply draw attention to the two verbs which precede and follow the proclamation of the kingdom here. 'Is fulfilled' (*peplērōtai*) looks backwards, as we have already noted. 'Is at hand' (the RSV translation nicely captures the ambiguity of *ēngiken*) connects the present significant moment with the future. In a similar way the gospel summary of Mark 1:15 as a whole is connected to antecedent Scripture via the introductory

---

[30] Eg G. North and G. DeMar, *Christian Reconstructionism. What it is, what it isn't* (Tyler, Texas: The Institute for Christian Economics, 1991). For a review of reconstructionism see R. Clapp, 'Democracy as Heresy (reconstructionist theology)', *Christianity Today* 31 (1987), 17–23. For an example of ethical reflection which (hopefully) avoids this problem, see my article, 'The Relevance of the Old Testament for Christian Social Ethics', in *Explorations 3. Christians in Society* (ed B. G. Webb; Sydney: Lancer, 1988), 113–130.

'as it is written' of 1:2, and to subsequent Scripture by the way
it is foundational to the NT gospel as whole (again as we have
seen). In other words, the gospel summary of Mark 1:15 is no
more separable from Scripture as a whole than the events of
the gospel are separable from the events of salvation history.
With this in mind I want to reflect more generally at this point
on the hermeneutical implications of the fact that the gospel
affirms in the strongest possible terms the rule of God. What
will be the effect if this central gospel affirmation is allowed to
shape biblical interpretation?

The first and most fundamental effect will be to deliver the
interpretive process from what we may call hermeneutical
idolatry. Most surveys of post-Enlightenment hermeneutics
trace the shift from an early author-centred approach to a
subsequent text-centred approach to a current reader-centred
approach. In line with this shifting focus, the perceived goal of
hermeneutics has changed from engagement with the mind of
the original author or authors to engagement with the text
without reference to the intentions of the author (which are
held to be irrecoverable) to what is basically engagement with
oneself, the text functioning as a kind of catalyst for self-
expression and self-discovery. All of these approaches have
something to teach us, and none of them is to be dismissed out
of hand. But viewed in the light of the gospel all of them are
exposed as basically idolatrous. Each in its own way wrests
Scripture from God, and hermeneutics from dependence on
God. But the gospel Jesus preached was 'the gospel of God'
(Mark 1:14) and its central theme was the rule of God (Mark
1:15), and inasmuch as Scripture has the same essential character, the goal of hermeneutics is engagement with God. The
implications for the praxis of hermeneutics are great, and we
will only be able to begin to explore them in this paper, but any
approach to hermeneutics which does not begin, continue and
end with acknowledgment of God and dependence on him
cannot be said to be evangelical.

The second effect will be to commit the interpreter to the
belief that absolute truth exists and is in principle accessible to
us. The major challenge of postmodernism is its denial of this.
There is simply no escape from the absolute sovereignty of the

subjective or the metaphorical nature of language. All truth,
inasmuch as it exists at all, is existential and personal. But the
gospel proclamation of the kingdom of God challenges this at
its very core by affirming, among other things, the existence of
a reality which transcends not only the subjectivity of the
reader, but also the relative objectivity of the author and the
text, and that this absolutely objective reality has drawn near
(become accessible to us) in Jesus Christ. The new hermeneutic
has given us a salutary reminder of the unavoidably subjective
dimension to every act of interpretation. Our grasp of absolute
truth will always be imperfect, and subject to correction by
others who have grasped it more adequately than ourselves.
But the interpreter guided by the gospel will understand that
the subjective is itself subject to the sovereignty of God and that
therefore real access to objective truth is possible.

Evangelical hermeneutics and repentance
At this point we pass beyond the gospel itself to the imperatives
which follow it: 'repent and believe'.

'Repent' is strongly nuanced by the preceding context, in
which there has been reference to the prophetic ministries of
Isaiah and John the Baptist, the latter specifically preaching a
'baptism of repentance for the forgiveness of sins' (1:2–4).
Against this background we must conclude that *metanoias* has a
similar force to the OT *Goaō*, namely, wholehearted return to
God with a renunciation of all forms of behaviour inconsistent
with covenant obligations. And it carries with it the promise of
forgiveness, that is, restored relationship with God. But in verse
15 this general concept is brought into direct contact with the
gospel, which announces the arrival of a special moment in
salvation history. This refines the content of repentance and
gives it a particular new covenant focus.

The message of verse 15 is an indivisible whole. The parallelism of 'repent' and 'believe' complements the preceding
parallelism of 'the time is fulfilled' and 'the kingdom of God is
at hand'. The essential form that repentance takes in the new
situation which has arrived with the coming of 'Jesus Christ,
the Son of God' (1:1) is believing the announcement that the
promise of the coming kingdom of God has found its fulfilment

in him.[31] It is this which now brings with it the assurance of forgiveness of sins and the prospect of a life lived in covenant relationship with God.

In a sense this returns us to the point from which we set out, for it is precisely such a response to the gospel which is the presupposition of an evangelical hermeneutic. The evangelical is someone who has repented in this sense, whose whole approach to Scripture has been shaped by the belief in the gospel which it entails. But at the same we have been brought to the end point of our inquiry. For inasmuch as they flow out of the gospel indicatives, the imperatives point to the effects which the gospel is intended to produce, namely, a life lived in submission to the will of God as expressed in the gospel. Repentance is both the starting point and the goal of evangelical hermeneutics.

Some of the implications for the actual practice of hermeneutics have already been touched on in the previous section, namely, the obligation to avoid hermeneutical idolatry. Idolatry, whatever form it takes, needs to be recognised for the sin it is and repented of. However, one particular implication warrants special mention, and it relates to the current fashion of treating the text as a field on which various games can be played according to different rules, rather than a piece of communication which demands a particular response from the reader.[32]

The double imperative of Mark 1:15, 'repent, and believe', makes it quite clear that the gospel summarised in the previous two indicatives is not a neutral linguistic field, but a piece of communication intended to elicit a quite specific response. This

---

[31] The RSV's 'believe in the gospel' reflects the somewhat unusual construction pisteuvein ejn. Some (eg Lohmeyer, Marxsen, Ambrosiac) have given ejn its full weight in the sense of 'believe on the basis of the gospel', with what is believed being inferred from the context. But since to believe *on the basis of* the gospel effectively means to believe what the gospel declares to be the case, ie to believe the gospel, very little is at stake exegetically. For a brief discussion see Guelich, 45.

[32] This idea, which owes much to the philosophical work of Ludwig Wittgenstein in the 1950s, was placed firmly at the centre of hermeneutical discussion in the 1970s by John Dominic Crossan. See his article 'A Metamodel for Polyvalent Narration', *Semeia* 9 (1977), 105–147.

intention belongs not just to the immediate utterer of the words (in this case Jesus himself), but to the God who has sent him, and whose gospel it is: 'Jesus came into Galilee, preaching the gospel of God, and saying . . . "Repent . . .".' Furthermore, the context makes the link between the intentionality of the NT gospel and that of the OT scriptures, which embody the preaching of the prophets. The coming of the forerunner John the Baptist and, by implication, of Jesus himself, takes place 'As it is written in Isaiah the prophet' (v 2). In fact this same kind of intentionality pervades Scripture as a whole. The apostle John draws his own written account of the gospel towards its conclusion with the words, 'These are written that you might believe that Jesus is the Christ, the Son of God' (John 20:31). Compare also the preface to Luke's gospel (Luke 1:1–4), and the great lengths Paul goes to in Romans to make his gospel assertions clear and to call for appropriate response from his readers.[33] In short, Scripture has an intentional character grounded in the intentionality of the gospel itself.

It follows that to treat the Bible as a pure art object to be simply enjoyed or reacted to rather than understood is to fundamentally misread it.[34] It constitutes a deliberate evasion of the repentance that the Bible calls for. A repentant hermeneutic will be sensitive to the aesthetic qualities of Scripture as indicators of intention, but be committed to a communication model of hermeneutics rather than a games model.[35] It will not play games with the text.

---

[33] Eg the exhortations of Rom 6, following the assertions of ch 5, or the appeal of Rom 12:1,2, following the exposition of election and grace in chs 9–11.

[34] See K. J. Vanhoozer, 'The Semantics of Biblical Literature: Truth and Scripture's Diverse Literary Forms', *Hermeneutics, Authority and Canon* (ed D. A. Carson & J. D. Woodbridge; Grand Rapids: Zondervan, 1986), 49–104. Vanhoozer argues that, given the propositional intent of Scripture, to pursue the intended meaning is not only possible but necessary. There is an ethical mandate that we do so.

[35] For an introduction to speech-act theory and a communication model of hermeneutics see the seminal works of J. L. Austin, *How to Do Things with Words* (Oxford: Oxford University Press, 1962) and J. R. Searle, *Speech Acts* (Cambridge: Cambridge University Press, 1969).

Final reflections

Much, much more could be said, and needs to be, if all the elements of an authentically evangelical hermeneutic are to be identified and set in their proper relationships to one other. All that the present constraints of time and space will permit, however, are some brief comments on three issues which require further work. They lie beyond the strict parameters set here, but are of such importance that it would be remiss of me to close without flagging them as essential agenda items for the ongoing discussion to which I hope this volume will give fresh impetus.

Hermeneutics and the Holy Spirit

The NT as a whole makes it clear that the Holy Spirit is indispensable in bringing about the response ('repent, and believe') which the gospel is intended to elicit. The Spirit transforms natural people into spiritual people capable of understanding and receiving spiritual things, namely, the truths of the gospel (1 Cor 2:14,15). Paul's gospel preaching, inasmuch as it has this effect on people, is a demonstration of the Spirit's power (1 Cor 2:4). The remarkable transformation in the formerly pagan Thessalonians is attributed to the fact that 'they received the word . . . with joy inspired by the Holy Spirit' (1 Thess 1:6). And the movement from preached gospel to written Scripture is undergirded by the promise that the Spirit will lead the apostles into all truth (John 16:12–15). So fundamental is the Spirit's role in this process that 'all scripture' (an expression which in context links the new with the old) can appropriately be described as 'God-breathed' (*theopneustos*), effectively the speech of God. Consequently the work of the Spirit is as indispensable in enabling people to respond to Scripture as in enabling people to respond to the gospel.

This clearly has profound implications for a gospel-based hermeneutic, especially as it seeks to position itself in the context of contemporary discussion. As we have already touched on above, a fundamental premise of a great deal of current hermeneutical theory is that there is an unbridgeable gap between author and the text. In the act of writing, the text is separated from the author and assumes a life of its own, quite independent of him. But the connection between the gospel, the Spirit and Scripture we have just noted effectively closes this gap. God and his gospel are never separated; word and Spirit are inextricably joined together. This is why an evangelical hermeneutic must have an epistemology which acknowledges the key role of the Spirit.[36] In terms of hermeneutical practice it means that evangelicals will begin, continue, and end their interpretive endeavours with prayer. We may not have direct access to the immediate authors (the biblical writers) but we do to the ultimate author. In prayer we acknowledge that, finally, God is his own interpreter,[37] and we need the help of his Spirit to safeguard us against our sinfulness and to grant us the illumination necessary to rightly understand and respond to divine truth.

Hermeneutics and community

One major effect of the gospel is to create a community of believing people, and this means that an evangelical hermeneutic cannot afford to ignore the mutual dependence we have on one another as well as on God himself. Furthermore, since the

---

[36] For some helpful recent discussion see Carson, *The Gagging of God*, 266–268; F. H. Klooster, 'The Role of the Holy Spirit in the Hermeneutic Process: The Relationship of the Spirit's Illumination to Biblical Interpretation', *Hermeneutics, Inerrancy and the Bible* (ed E. D. Radmacher & R. D. Preus; Grand Rapids: Zondervan Academie, 1984), 451–472; R. B. Zuck, 'The Role of the Holy Spirit in Hermeneutics', *Bibliotheca Sacra* 141 (1984), 120–130; J. Veenhof, 'The Holy Spirit and Hermeneutics', *The Challenge of Evangelical Theology: Essays in Approach and Method* (ed Nigel M. de S. Camerson; Edinburgh: Rutherford House, 1987), 39–57; G. D. Fee, *Gospel and Spirit. Issues in New Testament Hermeneutics* (Peabody, Massachusetts, 1991); Thomas F. Torrance, 'The Epistemological Relevance of the Holy Spirit', *Ex auditu verbi. Bundel voor G. C. Berkouwer* (ed R. Schippers et al; Kampen, 1965), 272–296; L. Hart, 'Hermeneutics, Theology, and the Holy Spirit', *Perspectives in Religious Studies* 14 (1987), 53–64.

[37] V. S. Poythress, 'God's Lordship in Interpretation', WTJ 50 (1988), 27–64. Significantly, apart from theologically insignificant uses (eg John 1:38,42) the only occurrences of the eJrmhneuvw word group in the NT associate interpretation with either Jesus (Luke 24:27) or the Holy Spirit (1 Cor 12:10; 14:26, 28).

Spirit is given to all believers, not just to a professional elite, the experts can no more afford to ignore the contribution of non-professionals than vice versa. This is not to deny the essential role of leadership by those gifted for it, but to recognise that responding to the gospel (which is what evangelical hermeneutics is) is foundational to the life of the people of God as a whole and that to do it properly we need to submit to and learn from one another. The gospel demands humility. We cannot afford to be arrogant.

Hermeneutics and general revelation

Finally, does the insistence that a gospel-based understanding of the nature of Scripture is essential if we are not to misread it mean that evangelicals have nothing to learn from those who do not share their evangelical faith? I think not; indeed many of the insights of this paper have been derived from interaction with people with whom I would fundamentally disagree at the level of their basic presuppositions about the nature of the Bible.

Here the OT wisdom literature is particularly instructive, for it holds in fine tension an insistence that 'the fear of Yahweh is the beginning of knowledge' (Prov 1:8), with a judicious policy of accepting and valuing the valid insights of non-Israelite sages.[38] In short, there is an implicit recognition in this literature that such people can have true knowledge of many particulars. What they lack is a knowledge of God himself, and therefore a framework into which to fit the particulars so that they add up to a true world view. In similar fashion we may hold that the gospel is the beginning of hermeneutics without unnecessarily impoverishing ourselves by cutting ourselves off from the wider hermeneutical debate. This, too, requires humility, but also a

---

[38] Eg the sayings of 'Agur son of Jakeh of Massah' and 'Lemuel, king of Massa' (Prov 30:1; 31:1), and, more generally, 'the words of the wise' in Prov 22:17–24:22 which parallels in many respects the Egyptian text, *The Instruction of Amen-em-opet*, which almost certainly predates it. See J. B. Pritchard (ed), *The Ancient Near East, Volume I. An Anthology of Texts and Pictures* (Princeton: Princeton University Press, 1958), 237–243. Similarly note how, while Solomon's wisdom is said to surpass that of non-Israelite sages, their wisdom is implicitly acknowledged (1 Kgs 4:29–31).

clear understanding (if we are not to fall into unprincipled eclecticism) of what an authentically evangelical hermeneutic is. Hopefully this paper has made a contribution to furthering such an understanding.

Exploring further

1. Does the proposition that such a thing as evangelical hermeneutics exists imply that there is only one correct interpretation of any particular Bible passage? Why or why not?
2. In what ways should an evangelical display humility in interpreting the Bible?
3. Are you comfortable with the idea that biblical hermeneutics is an 'art' rather than a 'science'? Why or why not?
4. What is the difference between evangelical interpretation of Scripture and proof-texting?
5. What is the importance, and what are the dangers, of emphasising the role of the Holy Spirit in biblical interpretation?

Teaching Doctrine as Part of the Pastor's Role

Peter Jensen

Synopsis

Although the various elements of the theological syllabus are separated for the purpose of instruction, the pastoral task requires integration. In particular, the reading and explanation of the Bible needs both biblical theology and doctrine. The thesis of this paper is that without biblical theology, doctrine is arbitrary; but without doctrine, biblical theology is ineffective. To establish this argument, methods of each discipline are described and attention is given to the reasons why the two disciplines need one another. The four vital tasks of doctrine are then outlined, with a plea that pastors take up the responsibility of preaching doctrinally so that their people may receive 'the whole counsel of God'.

Why we need doctrine

It is somewhat cheeky to write about our need of doctrine in a volume dedicated to biblical theology. Indeed, it is like attending a wedding with the rather loud ex-girlfriend of the groom as your uninvited partner. The desire to be free of doctrine gave the academic study of biblical theology its historical start, and to this day there are those who see the two disciplines as enemies or even mutually exclusive of one another. If we think of doctrine and systematic theology as roughly the same thing for the purpose of this discussion, it is clear that much modern doctrine is done with little regard to the theology of the Bible. It is true that there are biblical references in books of modern theology, and often an attempt to use some biblical concept, such as *koino | nia*, but there is little to suggest that it would be right to begin a sentence or settle an argument with the words 'The Bible says . . .' Systematic theologians are not given an agreed way of treating the Bible which will bring its teaching into fruitful and decisive contact with their own. The attempt to do so through the biblical theology movement of the mid-twentieth century is generally regarded as having failed. On the other hand, those who practise the exegesis and interpretation of the Bible tend to show disdain for the work of the systematic theologian. They observe with some justice that the theologian is frequently out of touch with the Bible, or that the appeal to the Bible is manifestly illegitimate. The words 'proof text' are especially damning.

The exclusion of one from another is damaging to both and damaging to the church. We need to recognise, of course, that our aim is to grow in the knowledge of God, so that we may love and serve him better. Doctrine and biblical theology are mutually dependent, and must be treated together if we are to understand the will and purposes of God. Unless biblical theology is the fundamental source and norm of doctrine, it will lose touch with the truth; likewise, biblical theology depends for its very existence on doctrine, and is not able to stand alone. My thesis is that without biblical theology, doctrine is arbitrary; but without doctrine, biblical theology is ineffective. There will be no satisfactory doctrine unless it is arrived at through biblical theology. There will be no satisfactory practical application of biblical theology unless the necessity of doctrine is attended to.

Relating biblical theology and doctrine

Themes and topics

Let us begin the discussion with some observations about how best to comment on a text, especially a biblical text. T. H. L.

Parker has provided a valuable introduction to this issue in his consideration of Calvin's methods.[1] He points out that other reformation commentators like Melanchthon, Luther and Bucer attempted to break open the meaning of the text by expounding topics which they found within it. He describes it as 'the searching out in a document of its teaching concepts, those which together comprehend the meaning of the whole'.[2] To refer to a readily accessible example, Luther's introduction to the epistle to the Romans consists of explanatory notes on a number of the key Pauline words and expressions, such as Law, Flesh, and Justification. He contrasts this with Calvin's method, which was to provide a continuous exposition of the text, commenting briefly as the material unfolded in its own order. In this way Calvin hoped to comment on the whole Bible, so that you could follow the story of the Scriptures, using his commentaries as a guide. For the sake of this discussion, I am going to refer to this method as 'thematic', with the idea that the procedure is accompanied by the discovery and following of themes as they unfold in the material.

Both methods are valid, and both lead to insights into the significance of the text. While Calvin's thematic method is rightly preferred by most contemporary biblical scholars, it would be foolish to neglect the usefulness of the topical approach. Indeed, Calvin himself did not regard his commentaries as capable of standing on their own. He was also at pains to provide a topical account of the Bible embodied in the *Institutes*. The *Institutes*, too, are an exposition of the Bible, but in a topical way. Indeed, this method is not merely valid, it is necessary if we are ever to make use of a text or group of texts. We legitimately ask, for example, for an explanation of the views of Freud or Marx, or Darwin or Bernard Shaw, or the Rabbis. The final truth about such questions can only be arrived at by a reading of the whole of their work in order. But if you wish to communicate the truth, if you wish to put the truth to work, you need to have it in a form able to be summarised, ordered, compared,

---

[1] T. H. L. Parker, *Calvin's New Testament Commentaries* (London: SCM, 1971), 26–48.

[2] Parker, 31.

analysed, remembered and transmitted. In short, you need it in a topical form.

To my mind, what we call biblical theology is very much in line with Calvin's thematic approach. But, as *biblical* theology, it is the application of the method to the whole Bible, not just the individual books. It fits with Graeme Goldsworthy's description:

> Biblical theology is concerned with God's saving acts and his word as these occur within the history of the people of God. It follows the progress of revelation from the first word of God to man through the unveiling of the full glory of Christ. It examines the several stages of biblical history and their relationship to one another. It thus provides basis for understanding how texts in one part of the Bible related to all other texts. A sound interpretation of the Bible is based on the findings of biblical theology.[3]

Packer on the theological disciplines

In a valuable article written for the volume in honour of R. E. Lucas, J. I. Packer gives an account of how the various theological disciplines relate to one another. He sees them as constituting ten 'linked disciplines', and enumerates them in order as, exegesis, biblical theology, historical theology, systematic theology, apologetics, ethics, spiritual theology, missiology, liturgy, and practical theology. Of these, he argues that systematic theology is the pivot. Indeed, he regards the last six (starting with apologetics) as aspects of systematics, individually treated for the sake of the syllabus, but integral to the task of systematics proper.

As can be seen from the list, Packer distinguishes biblical from systematic theology. He describes biblical theology as answering the question, 'What is the total message of the canonical books on this or that subject?', and says of systematic theology that it

> . . . rethinks biblical theology with the help of historical theology in order to restate the faith, topic by topic and as

---

[3]   G. L. Goldsworthy, *According to Plan* (Leicester: IVP, 1991), 37.

a whole, in relation to current interest, assumptions, questions, hopes, fears and uncertainties in today's church and world.[4]

He subsequently points out that the main topics of systematic theology are seven in number: revelation, God, man, Christ, the Holy Spirit, the church, and the future. The topics provide the structure for many text-books in systematic theology, especially from the Reformed perspective.

There is obviously much here which is valuable. We need to inquire, however, whether Packer has sufficiently distinguished biblical from systematic theology in its methodology. 'The total message of the canonical books on this or that subject', is not sufficiently distinguished from the topical approach which is the groundwork of systematic theology. Biblical theology in the sense described by Goldsworthy provides an indispensable intermediate step on the way to systematic theology. The consequence of accepting the Packer proposal is that the necessity of a thematic approach to the Bible as a prior step is not recognised, and that it does not, therefore, find a place in the theological syllabus. Whether the solution is to include both methods under the heading of biblical theology or to reserve the topical approach to systematic theology is a secondary issue. But unless a role is consciously assigned to the developmental approach, it will be omitted, to our loss.

The loss of not using biblical theology, so understood, may be summarised under three points. First, the interpretation of individual texts is affected by the presence or absence of biblical theology. The effect of biblical theology is that the interpretation of the parts is brought into connection with the understanding of the whole as the whole is developing. It is not sufficient to expound a psalm, for example, without stepping back from the exegesis of the particular in order to consider the flow of the whole, the place of the psalm in the ongoing revelation of the word of God. The theological content of the psalm feeds into the topical understanding of the Bible via its place in the development of the revelation. Biblical theology is indispensable to the task of comparing Scripture with Scripture.

---

[4] J. I. Packer, *When God's voice is heard* (Leicester: IVP, 1995), 80.

Second, without biblical theology, the appeal by a topically based systematic theology is distorted. It will have a tendency to display one of two errors. On the one hand, evangelicals will be prone to unprincipled appeal to texts which seem to bear on the topic under review, but which are taken out of their context in the Bible as whole. We may judge, for example, that the common manner of treating the ten commandments by evangelicals has fallen into this trap. On the other hand, there is the even worse problem exhibited by many theologically liberal thinkers. Since they do not begin from a doctrine of inspiration, and cannot therefore hold to the unity of Scripture, there is no way in which they are capable of creating a theology of the whole Bible. At most we see theologies of the Old or New Testaments. The lack of a coherent view of the whole Bible means, however, that the theological appeal to the Bible will be highly selective. The orthodoxy of many systematic theologians on matters such as the Trinity, therefore, seems to rest on the church tradition rather than any ability to read the doctrine from the Bible, notwithstanding the fact that the tradition itself was shaped by the Scriptures read in that way.

Third, without biblical theology the topics chosen by the systematic theologians as the basis of their work lack complete biblical reality. They are intended to focus the Bible's teaching on several highly significant areas of the Bible's interest. But, when considered from the viewpoint of our knowledge of the Bible through biblical theology, the characteristic order of treatment is unhelpful, the connections between the topics is unclear, and their significance is misunderstood. These assertions are most easily able to be demonstrated with regard to eschatology. What Packer refers to as 'the future' and places at the end of the list of topics, has a rather different meaning and location in the Bible. The eschatology of the Bible impacts so dramatically on the present, that to relegate treatment of it to the future is to distort its significance. Furthermore, the eschatological purview of the Scriptures is so urgent, and so much part of the framework of the Bible's story, that it must find early consideration in systematic treatments of the biblical faith. One of the great consistent weaknesses of theologians of virtually all schools of thought is in their inability to expound the resurrection of Jesus in its theological significance.

To put the matter simply: the reason is a failure to give eschatology its place. We may also wonder aloud whether such time-honoured devices as treating the work of Christ under the rubric of 'prophet, priest and king' would survive due recognition of biblical theology. Other theological topics crying out for different treatment include the sterile discussions of the attributes of God, and the difficulties experienced in discussing regeneration, worship and sanctification.

Doctrine needs biblical theology

If Packer is right in his list of the topics of systematic theology, it is high time that the list and the order of the list was critically reviewed. Biblical theology would suggest that the proper starting point is eschatology itself, the biblical history in its seed, its flowering and its fruition. Unless we have this time framework we cannot truly appreciate what God has done, is doing and will do. To start with eschatology is to put the biblical doctrines into the context of ultimate things. Indeed, perhaps a better way of making the same point is to suggest that we start with the gospel itself, which is eschatological to its core, and contains within itself the great doctrines of creation, revelation, God, humanity, the Christ and the church which must later be unfolded. The gospel is both christological and eschatological; it provides in itself the very pattern of God addressing us in his word of promise which must dominate our concept of revelation; it deals with the resurrection in the right place, and it invites those trusting relationships which are the foundation of salvation and the life of faith. The old schema does not get near this dynamic; indeed, you can study theological textbooks of the most orthodox stamp which never discuss the basic question of what the gospel is or show by their structure or method of approach that they think that the gospel matters as such. Their interests are not really the interests of the Bible.

In short, the 'topical' method of approach to the Scriptures cannot be undertaken without the 'thematic' approach. It is biblical theology which helps to keep us from exegetical error and enables the theologian to assess the relative place which individual texts play in the pattern of the whole of biblical truth.

But, even more than that, it is biblical theology which helps establish the topics with which doctrine should be concerning itself. It is a failure to observe the significance of the thematic which has led to the rather abstract list which we see in various doctrinal handbooks.

Biblical theology needs doctrine

Biblical scholars have become very jealous of their prerogatives in the years since biblical and systematic theology were formally divided from one another. It has sometimes seemed as though doctrine was the enemy, imposing false categories on the text, ignoring sound exegesis, using an arbitrary collection of proof texts to create a Christianity far removed from the biblical, and being prey to alien philosophical notions. But systematic theology cannot be dismissed quite so easily. Indeed, Packer is surely right to assert that the theological enterprise itself pivots around systematics. There are three reasons why we may regard doctrine as indispensable to biblical theology.

First, the topical exploration of Scripture, although it is not complete on its own, is nonetheless a legitimate means of approaching a body of writings, and yields insights not available to other, more atomistic methods. When we wish to see the wholeness of the truth, the interconnectedness of the parts, the coherence of the subject matter and the relationship of this truth to other bodies of fact or opinion, it is best to take up those subjects or topics most clearly treated in the material and ask ourselves, 'What do these writings taken as a whole say about that?' Given that it is appropriate and necessary to compare Scripture with Scripture, systematic treatments enable us to bring the whole to the part in any given case, to compare the general with the particular. As a result, the particular is able to be interpreted in the light of the whole. But the action is reciprocal: we are also able by the use of such a summary to examine the contribution that is made to the whole through the careful exegesis of the parts. A topical approach also makes easier the indispensable appeal to historical theology which needs to inform our understanding of Scripture.

Second, whether biblical theologians are prepared to acknowledge it or not, their work is based on systematic categories such as the inspiration, canon, unity and sufficiency of Scripture. It is true, of course, that in modern treatments of the Bible many of these categories are explicitly denied by biblical scholars. The result is, however, that we are no longer dealing with the Bible as such, but with a collection of ancient texts, the borders of which are no longer clear. It is literature of ancient Israel which becomes the category, not a volume known as the Bible. It is not surprising that biblical theology is little practised, for theology presupposes a God who speaks and reveals himself, and a God who is self-consistent. In other words, a theology is presupposed in any biblical theology. If – as has been the case – there have been biblical theologians whose aim has been simply to describe the teaching of the Bible without any commitment to a theology of the Bible, they are self-deceived. The Bible only exists as a collection because of the belief that God speaks uniquely in its pages. If that belief is abandoned, the logical result is the one which in fact has occurred, namely the abandonment of biblical theology as such.

Third, biblical theology needs systematic theology in order to apply the word of God. The topical methods employed in doctrine is the way in which we put the truths revealed by biblical theology to work. We need those summary statements of the truth which enable us to say with confidence, 'The Bible says . . .' Packer's conviction that systematic theology is pivotal to the whole enterprise of understanding the Bible and using its teaching is absolutely correct. Systematic theology cannot consist of the mere restatement of biblical material, but must boldly venture into its task, in Packer's words, 'to restate the faith, topic by topic and as a whole in relation to current interest, assumptions, questions, hopes, fears and uncertainties in today's church and world'. Indeed, apologetics, liturgics, ethics and the rest are really parts of systematic theology rather than disciplines in their own right.

The Bible as doctrine

If we further pursue the question of why biblical theology is not adequate on its own, the clue is found in the concept of the doctrine of the Bible. That is, we have a legitimate interest in the teaching of the Bible as such, and to give a final answer to that question requires the resources that Christian doctrine can bring. It needs the procedure of topical investigation, of summary statements, of the testing by history and the application to the present which are characteristic of doctrine.

The older translations of the Bible had their references to 'doctors', as in 'doctors of the law' (Luke 2:46), and, over thirty times, to 'doctrine'. For example, there is 'every wind of doctrine' in Ephesians 4:14, and the inquiry of the first hearers of Jesus, 'What new doctrine is this?' (Mark 1:27). Jesus was thought of as a teacher, because that was so characteristic of his ministry. The contrast between Jesus and the teachers of the law caused comment. Although he was not accredited 'the people were astonished at his doctrine, because he taught as one who had authority' (Matt 7:28). The activity of teaching the word of God was amply provided for in the OT (eg Deut 4:1; 4:10; 24:8; Ezra 7:10), and the priests and prophets, with parents, were the teachers of Israel.

In the NT, teaching is the chief distinguishing mark of the ministerial activity. Of course, the content of the teaching may well have included what we may call biblical theology, but there was clearly more to it than that. Something more like the structured material that we associate with doctrine is in evidence. Accompanying the provision of teaching as an activity, there is a body of material which may be called 'the teaching': 'the teaching you have learned' (Rom 16:17); 'the form of teaching to which you were entrusted' (Rom 6:17); 'Watch your life and doctrine closely' (1 Tim 4:16). More ominously, there is a reference to 'false doctrine' (1 Tim 1:3). John warns, 'Anyone who runs ahead and does not continue in the teaching of Christ does not have God' (2 John 9). What these references reveal is that just as the activity of faith is grounded in 'the faith' (Jude 3), so the activity of teaching is linked to 'the teaching', a body of truths which convey the faith, which are the grounds of faith, which guard faith, which sustain faith.

There has been a tendency in the past to treat the Bible as though it is a text-book, that is, a teaching manual. This fails to do justice to the whole nature of the Bible and the relationship with God which it creates and sustains. Its poetry, its worship, the torment of some of its authors, its stories, its wisdom may not be best thought of as 'teaching' in the first instance. But it is also possible to overreact. God is a teacher; his Torah is instruction; one of the honoured titles of Jesus is 'teacher'; there is such a thing as Christian teaching which is drawn from the Bible and which accepts the Bible as its source and its norm. We are taught by the poetry, stories and wisdom of the Bible. Furthermore, when Paul writes, 'We know that an idol is nothing at all in the world and that there is no God but one' (1 Cor 8:4), he is encapsulating the teaching of the OT and passing it on to us. At this and other points in the NT we may see the sort of summarising teaching in which the faith was committed to others, not only in statements about God, but in such things as ethical instruction as well.

There is a further reason why doctrine is needed, and not merely biblical theology. In the formation of Christian doctrine we need to use all the resources which God has blessed us with. Not only do we consult exegesis and biblical theology, we need the original languages and reading skills. Nor do we work in a vacuum. We need to constantly consult the reading of others, who also have pored over the biblical text. Confessions of faith, the deliberations of councils, the writings of theologians and others are all part of an interpretative tradition which it would be as much folly to ignore as it would be to canonise. However, we need to go further than that. There have been grave crises in the affairs of the Christian church where the whole future of the faith was at stake doctrinally. At these moments, decisions have been taken about how the Scriptures are to be read if we are to be fair to the Bible as a whole. From then on Christianity has been committed to that reading of Scripture in so strong a way that any other reading cannot be sustained. Obviously I have in mind here the controversies over the Trinity and the two natures of Christ. If you were to choose, as the Jehovah's Witnesses have done, to read your Bible as saying that Christ is not fully God, you would be choosing no longer to be Christian; though, of course, in the final analysis you may (theoretically) be right, for even this tradition is not strictly canonical.

In short, a biblical theology which merely stopped short at itself would not in the end be effective, being unable to be assimilated and used by the listener. The findings of biblical theology must be gathered up and presented to the Bible reader in a way that the teaching of Scripture can be assimilated, remembered, reproduced and used. That way is doctrine. To simplify an illustration used by B. B. Warfield:

> exegesis summons the texts as soldiers are summoned for an army; biblical theology forms them up and allots each its proper place; doctrine gives the army its order to march against the foe.[5]

The uses of doctrine

Doctrine is the summary of the teaching of Scripture on its great topics in a way which reveals the relationship between the topics. It enables us to perform four vital tasks.

First, it enables us to understand the Bible. If it is true to say that the ultimate context of every text is the Bible, we need a way in which the whole Bible can be allowed to bear witness to the parts, and the parts speak to our understanding of the whole. Doctrine functions to allow this vital interchange to take place. Thus, for example, when we read about the face of God in the OT, we understand the phrase through the witness of the NT, which tells us that God is spirit. When we read about the righteousness of God's people we know that their righteousness is relative to the great fact of universal human sinfulness. When we read that Christ is the first born of all creation we read Paul in the knowledge that he himself bears witness to the divinity of Christ elsewhere. When we see an emphasis on human effort or on divine power, we remember the doctrinal rule garnered from other passages of Scripture that God and human effort work fully together without prejudice to either but with priority to God. A sound doctrinal understanding will hold tensions in the text without rushing to relieve them. It will throw light on obscurity in the individual passages.

---

[5] Warfield's illustration is cited by Carson, 'Unity and Diversity in the New Testament' in D. A. Carson and J. D. Woodbridge, *Scripture and Truth* (Grand Rapids: Baker, 1992), 70.

Second, doctrine enables us to remember the Bible. The Christian life is sustained by the Bible. The Scriptures themselves testify to the desirability of the assimilation of their message by reading, hearing, exposition, meditation, and other forms of learning. No book of doctrine can replace the Scriptures, not least because doctrinal understanding is not the only function of the Bible. But by arranging the message of Scripture in an orderly way, doctrine helps us to recall its teaching. It also assists in checking the accuracy of our understanding of Scripture, and opening us to further correction. It may have been the case in times past that churches with a confessional and catechetical bent have promoted doctrine at the expense of biblical theology and exegesis. But our current practice is very different, and we are in danger of losing what doctrine can and must give. Is it still the case in Sunday school that most of the time is spent on introducing children to the stories of the Bible? Doctrine must stand as the conceptual aid to the reading of the Bible, and in whatever suitable form it must be taught to children. Likewise our commitment to exposition must be accompanied in some way by the doctrine of Scripture if we do not want to leave people unable to remember, and hence unable to conceptualise and to use the faith which they are being taught.

Third, doctrine enables us to be discriminating Christians. We need to be able to identify who we are by what we believe. Long gone are the days when Christians could rely on ethnic characteristics to perform such a role. We can no longer rely on the liturgy to do the same; the loss of liturgical worship is a severe blow to the cause of doctrine. The fact of doctrine serves to draw Christians together in a common cause; hence the significance of the doctrinal basis for evangelical groups ministering on university campuses. At the same time, it serves to distinguish them from others and also to determine the relative importance of such divisions. Doctrine guards the purity of faith and keeps us in the way of truth. It enables the pastor to drive away falsehood and error. Doctrinal principles firmly adhered to will also protect us from such pragmatic activities as beguile us with their alleged fruitfulness. Doctrinal soundness will protect Christians from the seductions of the latest purveyors of experiential Christianity, thereby enabling them to rejoice in the true experiences of God and reject the experiences which do not accord with righteousness.

Fourth, doctrine enables us to apply the Bible. Doctrine stands on the border between the Bible and the world. It enables us to preach, to pray and to praise; it is the basis of work in ethics, apologetics, liturgy and pastoral theology. The minister of God's word, whether in public preaching or private counsel, must be an expert in Christian doctrine. Studies such as ethics need to stand ultimately on the integrated summary of the Christian faith which it is the business of doctrine to provide. They cannot remain with the consideration of the many passages of Scripture but require to be informed by the whole witness of Scripture. They need to be able to hold in appropriate tension the requirements of the different topics of Scripture. Thus, the doctrine of sin needs to be related to the nature of the atonement, and both are needed in the pastoral task of preaching the gospel of forgiveness and repentance. It is through doctrine, too, that comparison is made with other systems of belief, whether within or without the church.

Conclusion

It sometimes must appear that there exists a hierarchy of importance in the tasks done by professor of theology on the one hand and the pastor on the other, with the honours belonging to the professor. It seems that those who are engaged in the academic study of theology must have the more difficult task, and the greater wisdom. The task of the professor is indeed demanding and responsible, and it often requires a technical proficiency beyond the reach or need of the ordinary pastor. But we have gone far astray if we imagine that such a facility amounts to an advantage in honour to the professor.

The tasks of the pastorate in the modern world are multifarious. But whatever else pastors do, they must engage themselves in the preaching of the word of God, especially through the exposition of Scripture. This, above all, cannot be avoided or done poorly. When they stand before the congregation to expound the word of the Lord, they will require the greatest resources of intellect and spirit which it is possible to bring to any task. Far from preaching being easier than theological lecturing, for example, or writing a book, it is more demanding. The theological syllabus is divided into many sections so that the teachers may specialise; pastors have to re-assemble the whole syllabus and call on their understanding of the world they inhabit, in order to bring the word of the Lord to their people. The intellectual challenge alone is daunting.

Preaching is a great (though by no means the only) test of a pastor's theology. As those who have the chief human responsibility for ensuring that the Lord's people meet the Lord week by week, pastors must give themselves to being servants of the Lord's word. They must expound the Scriptures, teaching the Lord's people what the Lord says. Expository preaching first of all depends upon exegesis. But a sermon which is mere exegesis is no sermon. The part must be included in a wider whole; it needs the thematic study of biblical theology, and finally the topical study of doctrine if it is to do the job of relating the hearers to their proper responses to God in the world. The hearer must know in the end what the whole Bible says about the subject raised by the part under study. The skilled pastor is, therefore, an expert in all exegesis, in biblical theology and in doctrine.

The expertise of pastors is not for their own benefit. The more their hearers know the Bible, the more easily they can respond appropriately to the word of the Lord. Preaching may be the pastor's greatest task, but it will be weakened in its power if it is not accompanied by a careful program of Christian education for all members of the congregation. Calvin was a great preacher; he also taught through his thematic commentaries; but he also wrote his systematic theology so that the Lord's people would be fully instructed in the Bible. Preaching we do; in the modern parish the Bible study has become a characteristic small-group activity; where does doctrine fit in? If we are going to provide the necessary resources for God's people, we must reinstate doctrinal preaching in some assimilable form. In his day, the famous Richard Baxter did it through the door-to-door work of catechising his flock. How do we modern pastors intend to make sure that our hearers know the teaching that God has given us?

Exploring further

1. What is the connection between doctrinal truth and healthy faith?
2. Consider the place that doctrinal teaching should play in Christian education.
3. Should a preaching program contain doctrinal and ethical elements in addition to exposition?
4. Can historical theology contribute to the nurture of Christians?

Biblical Theology and Ethics
Michael Hill

Synopsis

A distinction is made between morality and ethics. Ethics involves the analysis and justification of morality. Christian ethics is seen to be an attempt to synthesise the bits and pieces of morality found in the Bible into a theory. Christian ethics is therefore an exercise in systematic theology. Biblical theology reveals that there is a progression in the revelation of God's plan and purpose. God has intermediate goals as well as a final goal. God does not go directly to the end. Any valid systematic use of the bits and pieces of morality must take into account the shape of salvation history. Systematic theology, and therefore ethics, needs to be based on biblical theology. While morality may not change in the course of the progressive revelation of God's purposes, the understanding of morality can and does. The content of morality may be fixed by the orders of creation and God's purposes, but the understanding of morality develops and changes as the purposes of God are revealed through the various stages of salvation history. Christian ethics finds its fullest exposition in the person and work of Christ. Ethical theories that ignore the role of biblical theology distort a true understanding of morality. Even those who endorse the role of biblical theology can highlight one stage over and above the others and so misconstrue the ethics of the Bible. Several examples are given.

Morality and the Bible

The Bible is full of morality. The ingredients are scattered throughout its pages. Moral rules, moral injunctions, and moral judgments abound. Moral virtues are explicitly adopted and promoted. For example, when Israel comes together as a people to proceed into the promised land they are given commandments which include the following moral rules:

> You shall not murder.
> You shall not commit adultery. (Exod 20:13–15)

Many of the moral rules are explicitly summed up as expressions of the principle 'love your neighbour as yourself' (Lev 19:18). Besides moral rules and principles we find lists of virtues and vices in the Scriptures.

> A righteous man cares for the needs of his animal. (Prov 12:10)
> Pride only breeds quarrels. (Prov 13:10)
> The acts of the sinful nature are obvious: sexual immorality, impurity and debauchery; idolatry and witchcraft; hatred, discord, jealousy, fits of rage, selfish ambition, dissensions, factions, and envy; drunkenness, orgies, and the like. I warn you, as I did before, that those who live like this will not inherit the kingdom of God. (Gal 5:19–21)
> But the fruit of the Spirit is love, joy, peace, patience, kindness, goodness, faithfulness, gentleness and self-control. (Gal 5:22,23)

Morality and ethics

Broadly speaking, ethics is the study of morality. In the study of ethics we begin with the descriptive task of trying to identify the moral standards and rules that people have adopted. Christians engage in the task of descriptive ethics when they study the Bible. For example, a person might go through the gospel of Mark and list all the moral rules, principles and values found there. As a consequence of this study the person would locate the morality of Mark's gospel. Descriptive ethics is not concerned to locate a set of values for people to live by but simply to locate the moral standards that people have or have had.

If the study of ethics is to be useful it must go beyond mere descriptive ethics. Christians study the Bible not just to know what moral standards the early Christians had but also to find a set of moral standards to live by in this modern world. The endeavour to find such standards is known as normative ethics. The task of normative ethics is to give an integrated account of moral values. Integrated accounts are called theories. Ethical theories attempt to explain the nature and unity of moral experience.

One aspect of the task of normative ethics is that of *analysis*. In normative ethics we analyse the rules, principles and values of a particular morality and see how all the parts or aspects fit together. Analysis will allow criticism of a particular morality but it will also lead to the next task, which is the task of *justification*. Justification is the task of demonstrating that we have the right values, principles and rules. That is, in normative ethics we attempt to show that a particular set of moral values meshes with reality in a way which is more adequate than other sets. In this way we attempt to vindicate our morality.[1]

None of the biblical writers set out to develop a theory of Christian ethics. The biblical writers had another agenda. They wanted to reveal what God was doing and saying in the world. Nevertheless these writers do record a lot of moral material. More than just recording moral matters, their theological insights give some clues about how that morality might be understood and integrated. These insights enable us to undertake the basic task of Christian ethics, which is to give an integrated account of morality as it is found in the Scriptures and provide a theory of ethics by which Christians may operate in their daily lives.

Evangelicals should not discount the need to develop an ethical theory based on the Bible. C. Stephen Layman, in his book *The Shape of the Good*, gives three reasons for developing an ethical theory.[2] Firstly, theories tell us the sort of thing we need to know to settle moral issues. This is especially true in a society like ours where traditional rules will not cover the situations generated by modern technology. Traditional rules

---

[1] In the case of Christian ethics justification will be in term of conformity to Scripture. Theological argument will be used to show that the right moral values have been located.

[2] C. Stephen Layman, *The Shape of the Good: Christian Reflections on the Foundations of Ethics* (Notre Dame: University of Notre Dame Press, 1991).

do not cover issues like sperm donation, surrogate mother-
hood, and the ozone layer. Secondly, theories present us with
a general picture or vision of the moral life. A theory will give
us a sense of the general direction we ought to be heading. This
sense can give us rough moral guidance and set the parameters
of our moral search and research. Thirdly, having a theory
helps us to be consistent and avoid bias. Frequently our capac-
ity for moral outrage is selective. We can be violently opposed
to abortion on demand and not concerned about an unjust war
in which our nation has some participation. Consistency is a
virtue.

The concern of this paper is to highlight the place biblical
theology has in the process of developing a Christian ethic.

The nature and shape of biblical theology

Evangelicals have always recognised the Bible as the word of
God. However, the recognition of the authority of the Bible does
nothing to answer the question of how the Bible is to be interpreted and understood. Can the bits and pieces which make up
the Bible be put together in any fashion? Or is the Bible like a
jigsaw puzzle where the size and the shape of the parts limit the
way the bits and pieces can be arranged? In this article our
concern is not just about any bits and pieces but about the bits
and pieces of morality. How can we put these together to develop a theory of Christian ethics which will help us to be faithful
to God's standards?

Many biblical scholars over the years have noted that the
Bible has a coherence and logic of its own.[3] The discipline of
biblical theology has grown out of this observation. Biblical
theology is an approach to Scripture which attempts to see the
biblical materials as a whole and to describe this wholeness in
biblical categories.[4] Fundamental to the unity of the Bible is the
fact that it reveals the activity of the one God who is saving a
people for himself within the process of history.

---

[3] For an interesting and revealing study of the history of biblical theology see
Charles H.H. Scobie, 'The Challenge of Biblical Theology' (Part 1), *Tyndale
Bulletin*, 42.1 (1991), 31–61.

[4] See Scobie, 50.

The history and logic contained in the Bible is complex. No one theme is adequate to describe the flow. Like an elaborate tapestry many colourful motifs are woven together to display an intricate design. However, study of the various themes have shown how 'the entire Bible is moving, growing according to a common purpose and towards a common goal.'[5] The common goal has been designated in different ways. The most common designation, and perhaps most apt, is the 'kingdom of God'. The use of the English word 'kingdom' in this phrase can be very misleading, for it tends to suggest a geographical domain. The biblical concept has more to do with the rule or reign of God. The essential idea is that of God establishing his order.[6]

Like all action within history God's actions in redeeming a people are sequential. Moreover, there is a definite pattern and shape to the sequence. Scobie identifies the elementary shape as proclamation, promise, fulfilment, and consummation.[7] Goldsworthy gives this basic promise/fulfilment pattern clear historical content.[8] The movement of salvation history is outlined as: the kingdom pattern established (Eden), the fall, the kingdom promised (Abraham), the kingdom foreshadowed (David, Solomon), the kingdom at hand (Jesus), and the kingdom consummated (the return of Jesus).

Biblical theology reveals that there is a progression in the revelation of God's plan and purpose. God has intermediate goals as well as a final goal. Indeed, the intermediate goals often point to and elucidate the final goal. God does not go directly to the end. There are a number of stages in God's unfolding plan, and biblical theology examines the relationships between these stages.

---

[5] W. J. Dumbrell, *The End of the Beginning: Rev 21–22 and the Old Testament*, (Grand Rapids: Baker, 1985), first page of the Introduction.

[6] While the term 'kingdom of God' does not occur in the Old Testament, and occurs infrequently outside the synoptic gospels in the New Testament, the concept of God's reign or rule is implicit from the very beginning of creation and is found under different terminology throughout the Scriptures.

[7] Charles H. H. Scobie, 'The structure of Biblical Theology', *Tyndale Bulletin*, Vol. 42.2, (November 1991), 187–194.

[8] G. L. Goldsworthy, *Gospel and Kingdom: A Christian Interpretation of the Old Testament* (Rydalmere: Crossroad edition, 1994), 49.

Biblical theology and systematic theology

If biblical theology seeks to understand the message of the
Bible taken as a whole, systematic theology brings together all
the biblical material on a topic and relates it to abiding human
interests as well as current concerns. We cannot put the bits
and pieces of biblical material on any given topic together in
any way we like. We are constrained by the sequential logic of
God's movement in history. In other words, biblical theology
plays an important and necessary intermediary role in moving
from the exegesis of particular passages and understanding
how those passages impact on us as Christians today. Any
theologising in the systematic sense which does not incorporate this intermediate step is not true to the logic and message
of the Bible.

The NT writers themselves advance a biblical theology. The
apostle Paul was making an important claim about the flow of
salvation history when he declared that Christians were not
under the law (eg Gal 5:18). The package of laws and customs
which gave shape to historical Israel as the people of God was
not to be applied to Christians. That package was outdated. A
new package had arrived with the person of Jesus. Christians
were 'in Christ' (eg 2 Cor 5:17; Rom 10:4).

While it was true that the law foreshadowed the shape of
things to be found in Christ, the law was an incomplete package.
This incomplete shape found its completion in Jesus (Matt 5:17;
Eph 1:3–10; Col 1:15–20). Christians were to look to Christ to see
the shape of God's rule. While it is necessary to study the law
and the prophets to understand the dimensions of the new
package in Christ, this does not place people under the old
package. To illuminate the new by the old is not to place oneself
under the old. This illumination is merely an educative process.
It helps one to understand the person and work of Christ.
Relevant aspects of the law were taken up in the person and
work of Christ. If aspects of the law are applicable, they are only
appropriate through Christ. Christ is now the operative unit.

Given the shape of biblical theology, systematic theology
cannot just gather together all the references to key topics such
as sacrifice and atonement in the Bible and give them the same

weight. If it did, then Christians would appear to be under the
command to offer animal sacrifice. Giving equal weight to OT
references on the topic of atonement would depreciate the
weight given to the sacrifice of Christ found in the NT and create
a tension between the Old and New Testaments. Such a doctrine
of the atonement would not be biblical.

Sacrifice and atonement can only properly be understood
within the framework of the various stages of salvation history
as recorded in the Scriptures. In Eden God provides a glimpse
of the goal or purpose that he has in mind. Adam and Eve walk
and talk with God in the garden. This heavenly fellowship was
broken by Adam and Eve's distrust and disobedience. Only
against this background of sin do sacrifice and atonement make
any sense. In moving to restore fellowship God uses a man of
faith to establish a people who will model God's kingdom. In
placing itself under God's rule Israel becomes the agent by
which God achieves his goal. The faithlessness and failure of
Israel highlights the point that Israel only foreshadowed God's
reign. God knew it could not be otherwise. The people of Israel,
like the rest of humanity, were slaves to sin. While the 'blood of
bulls and lambs' could anticipate the sacrifice of Christ and so
effect forgiveness of sins, it could not renew human nature. The
shadow anticipated the reality, and reflected the shape of the
reality, but it could not fill out the details. Nor did the shadow
have the power of the reality.

Biblical theology and biblical morality

While there is an obvious progression of God's revelation in
regard to sacrifice and atonement in the Scriptures, this does not
seem to be the case in regard to morality. Certain moral imperatives are common to all the stages of salvation history. Adultery,
for example, is wrong in both the Old and New Testaments.
These common moral imperatives suggest that the content of
morality does not change from stage to stage in salvation history.

There is some moral material, however, that does appear to
express change. For example, the moral imperatives in relation
to the interwoven themes of sex and marriage include some
apparently contradictory elements. The unity of marriage is both

proclaimed and modelled in Eden (Gen 2:18–25). Yet Moses
allows divorce (Deut 24:1–4). The prophet Malachi declares that
God hates divorce (Mal 2:16). Jesus reports that Moses only
allowed divorce because of Israel's hardness of heart (Matt
19:7–9). In some cases Jesus goes so far as to equate divorce with
adultery. However, he also proclaims that there will be no giving
and receiving in marriage at the consummation of God's rule
(Matt 22:23–33).

Importantly, these apparent changes in morality can be explained in terms of biblical theology. The moral norm of marital
fidelity and unity displayed in the creation accounts is the one
maintained in the kingdom under Christ. Marital fidelity is an
essential aspect of the lives of those who minister the gospel
(Titus 1:6). However, in the stage where Israel foreshadows
God's rule in Christ the people of Israel were slaves to sin. God
commands Moses to regulate their sinful behaviour in order to
limit the harm that might ensue. At this point in salvation history
Moses was operating on a retrieval ethic and not presenting the
ethical ideal. The sin which defeated the ideal is itself van-
quished in the work of Christ, where Christians die to sin and
rise again to righteousness. Paul hints that in the consummation
at the return of Christ the intimate sexual knowledge of marriage
will be replaced by a new way of knowing that is not sexual
(1 Cor 13:12). The intimacy which is now only found in marriage
will be extended to all relationships.

Biblical theology and Christian ethics

Christian ethics attempts to apply the bits and pieces of morality
found in the Bible to our contemporary lives. In this sense Christian ethics is an aspect of systematic theology. In developing an
account of how all the moral material in the Bible hangs together
we have to go beyond biblical theology. While elaborating a
Christian theory of ethics is the task of systematic theology,
biblical theology will place important constraints on the way the
task is done. To take a section of the OT which contained a range
of moral injunctions and apply them directly to contemporary
Christian life would not be adequate or truly biblical. A Christian
understanding of OT morality requires that it be evaluated in

relation to the work of Christ. Sections of OT morality cannot be isolated from the flow of salvation history and applied directly.

Paul's perspective on the use of OT commandments is a case in point. The commandments against adultery, murder, stealing, and coveting are applied to the Christian (Rom 13:8–10) but only in the context of theologising about the power of the gospel (Rom 1:16) and its outworking in the life of the Christian. The argument is that because love does no harm to its neighbour the commandments are summed up in the rule: love your neighbour as yourself. But love is not limited to the negative function of not doing harm. Love overcomes evil with good (Rom 12:9–21). In meeting evil in such a positive way Christian love imitates the love of God. God demonstrated 'his love for us in this: While we were still sinners, Christ died for us' (Rom 5:8). Within the flow of the argument of Romans it is made clear that Christians are able to love because they have been transformed by the renewing of their minds (Rom 12:2). This transformation has been accomplished through the cross of Christ. United to Christ by faith, Christians have died to sin and been made alive to God (Rom 6:1–4). Christ's death and resurrection has become theirs.

The dramatic emphasis on love in Pauline thought is captured by Galatians 5:6. Arguing against Judaisers who want to return to the package of Mosaic law, Paul declares 'the only thing that counts is faith expressing itself through love'. However, love is not portrayed as an end in itself anywhere in the NT. Rather, love is the lubricant and operating principle of the new community 'in Christ'. The community of God sighted in Eden and tasted by Adam and Eve before the fall is now present through the work of Christ. Living in an alien world and still fighting against the power of sin, the form of God's community is established but it awaits consummation. The NT writers continually remind us to consider the flow of salvation history and its significances for those 'in Christ'.

The flow of salvation history and the nature of morality

An outline of the moral and ethical aspects of the unfolding biblical drama will justify the development of a coherent overall theory. The creation accounts in Genesis 1–3 provide the grounds for belief in universal values based on the bedrock of an objective reality. In the act of creation God gives an order to things. This order is constituted by kinds and purposes.[9] Diverse kinds of things are brought into being. There are cattle and creeping things, birds and fishes, grass and trees. No complete list of the manifold kinds is given, but it is clear that one could classify or order creation into kinds. Another type of order is mentioned. This is the relationships between the kinds. For example, certain kinds of green plants are given as food to all the birds and animals. In the order of things these green plants are to serve as food. In this and many other instances indications are provided that there is an overall purposive order to creation in the way the kinds are related to one another.

When God created Adam and Eve they were created in God's image. The Hebraic notion of 'image' indicates that they were given dominion over creation. Acting as God's vice-regent they were to maintain the order God has created. In God's creational order nature and purpose go together. When we declare that slavery is immoral we are saying that people are the kinds of things that ought not to be treated in a certain fashion. People have knowledge, insight, and will, and can set their own agendas. God has a goal or purpose for people and this is reflected in their nature. They are not to be treated like dumb beasts. In the end we discover that God has given humans their specific nature so that they might enjoy certain kinds of relationships. Later in the NT we discover that these relationships are to be mutual love relationships. Human nature and God's purpose for humans go together and define each other.

Morality is objectively based. It arises out of creation's order and has to do with the value given to kinds. The value of a kind has to do with its own nature and its relationship to other kinds. Green plants have the value of food to animals. Other things like rocks, for example, cannot have the value of food. Eating a rock will not sustain an animal. Values are something we as subjects

---

[9] In more technical parlance kinds and purposes are referred to as generic and telic order. For a thorough discussion of the issue see Oliver O'Donovan, *Resurrection and Moral Order; An Outline for Evangelical Ethics*, (IVP: Leicester, 1986), chapter 2.

give to things. They are not found out there in the world like plants and animals. Nevertheless moral values cannot be arbitrarily given; they depend on the nature of the things involved.

The advent of sin and the rejection of God's order sees the establishment of a special people who live in a designated land. As God's people the children of Israel are required to reflect the character of God by living in his way and maintaining his order and purposes. Israel is intended to model God's order and be a witness to the world. In the revelation of the Torah to Moses some of God's purposes are spelt out in detail. Besides aspects of the moral law cultic issues are canvassed. The issue of sin is addressed. An essential element in the concept of sin is the idea of falling short of the goal that God has set. Sin is the wilful rejection of God's purposes and standards and as such ruptures relationship with God. Cultic aspects of the Torah have to do with how sinful people might approach a holy God. Procedures for the atonement of sin are laid down. The existence of the cult affirms the fact that Israel, as a model, points to something greater.

The words of the prophets speak to an Israel who persists in faithlessness and disobedience. Israel is continually called back to the terms of the covenant as expressed in the Torah. The major prophets frequently were called the ethical prophets by biblical scholars. One reason for this is exposed if we examine the notion of disobedience. Disobedience can disclose itself in two ways. An individual can reject God's particular will for them. Abraham, for example, could have refused to go to the promised land. A second form of disobedience does not involve God's particular will for specific individuals but God's will for kinds. Involving the kinds in creation and purposes of creation this general will of God is embedded in creation and incumbent upon all people. The obligations that arise out of this general will are moral obligations. The prophets reminded Israel of these moral responsibilities.[10]

From the fall onwards human nature is marred and God's purpose is unrealised. The true dimensions of humanity and the

---

[10] For example, the prophet Amos raises the issues of social abuse, class distinction, and the oppression of the poor.

goal that God intended for humankind have been cloaked behind the distortion of sin. There is a semblance of what might have been, but the picture is fractured and deformed. There is enough in the picture for the person of faith to confirm the command of God. Murder, adultery, and coveting all remain immoral, but any intellectual rationalisation that might explain and justify morality remain inadequate. This defect is repaired in the person of Jesus Christ. He is the true Israel. The true nature of humanity appears in him. He is the final state of things. His nature is love and he shares right relationships with the Father and all who trust in him.

The true and complete nature of love is shown only on the cross. Jesus is the true man. He is the one unique model of what everyone should be. In him is found the kind of person that we all should be. Christians are called to imitate Jesus, not in the sense of copying his life and ministry but in the sense of humble self-giving service. The magnitude of his self-giving love is found in the fact that he is willing to suffer and die for others in faithful obedience to his Father. Moreover, not only is Jesus perfect in kind but he accomplishes the purpose of God in relations, not only to humanity but the whole of creation. Mutual love relationships between God and humans and between human beings become a reality through his work. The power of God is found in the preaching of the gospel. Through the Spirit of God Christians die to sin and rise again to righteousness. By the forgiveness of sins Christians are freed to love God and serve their neighbour.

Throughout the movement of salvation history the content of morality has remained the same. In this sense the ten commandments are timeless. What was immoral is still immoral. Nevertheless the full dimensions of morality are only revealed in the person and work of Christ, because a comprehensive ethic can only be developed when the goal of creation has been unveiled. Ethics as a rationale for morality is only possible when the schema of salvation history is concluded. A complete analysis, understanding, and justification of the moral domain only comes with the revelation of the meaning of Christ's death and resurrectio n. Murder can now be seen as the opposite of self-giving service. Self-giving service is now justified in terms of the joy of mutual love relationships with both God and neighbour. Moreover, true morality is now possible because people have been released from slavery to sin.

Traps to avoid

Outlining the shape of salvation history is not enough to secure a valid biblical ethic. The question of focus and the weight given to the various stages of revelation can still be an issue. John Murray in his well-known book *Principles of Conduct* explicitly adopts what he calls 'the biblico-theological method'.[11] He defines biblical theology, following Geerhardus Vos, as 'that branch of Exegetical Theology which deals with the process of the self-revelation of God deposited in the Bible'.[12] He understands 'progressive revelation' to mean 'that revelation has a history of increasing and accumulating disclosure until it reaches its finale in the manifestation of the Son of God and the inscripturation in the complete NT canon'.[13] Nevertheless his focus is on creation and what he calls the 'Creation Ordinances'. These ordinances include marriage, labour, the sanctity of life and truth.

The movement of Murray's method is not the same as the movement of salvation history and biblical theology. Instead of moving from orders of kind to the final purpose revealed in Christ, one gets the impression that Murray reaches out and draws everything back into creation, the inference being that creation is seen to be intelligible in its own light. While this assessment may be a little harsh, there is no doubt that the focus is predominantly on creation. The subsequent movement in the Bible is seen to be contained in the framework of creation. Hence he is able to declare that 'the ten commandments . . . furnish the core of biblical ethics'.[14]

Yet the movement of biblical theology suggests that sin is not just the failure to obey a list of rules but the failure to be like Christ. The love of Christ displayed on the cross cannot be

---

[11] John Murray, *Principles of Conduct* (Grand Rapids: Eerdmans, 1957), 7.
[12] Murray, 7.
[13] Murray, 8.
[14] Murray, 7.

reduced to not murdering, committing adultery, stealing, lying, coveting or whatever else. The commitment to the good of others exhibited there is much much stronger and more positive than a reticence to do evil. When Paul declares that 'love fulfils the law' he does not imply that love is limited to doing no harm. Christian love is founded on the love Christ displayed on the cross. It is a profound commitment to the good of others.[15] Christians fulfil their moral obligations by participating in the love of Christ through dying and rising with him. Christian ethics is not captured and cannot be captured by obedience to a limited set of rules.

Another distortion of biblical ethics comes from focusing on the kingdom as it is in the consummation and ignoring the fact that Christians live between the fulfilment and the consummation. The contortions inflicted on biblical morality and ethics by this limited focus can be illustrated if we return to the issue of sex and marriage discussed in section five above. If the shape of reality in the consummated kingdom presents the moral ideal under which Christians are now to operate, then the male/ female order providing the basis of sexual morality is dismissed. In the consummated kingdom there is no giving and receiving in marriage. However, the NT writers uphold the order of creation in this present age. It will be transformed at the return of Christ. In the meantime the sexual order of male and female finds its fulfilment in marital fidelity.

A similar distortion can occur in theology when the flow of salvation history is ignored. It is true that mutual love relationships in heaven will be perfect. There will be no place for and no need of repentance and forgiveness in heaven. Nevertheless the NT writers highlight the ongoing need of repentance and forgiveness in the Christian community while it awaits the return of its Lord. The ideal cannot be directly achieved in the time between fulfilment and consummation. Many forms of perfectionism ignore the eschatological sequence of salvation history as it presents itself in biblical theology and so distort the biblical ethic.

---

[15] Of course, the good is determined on the basis of the order established at creation but only in the light of the purposes God has for that order.

Christian ethics and retrieval ethics

Christians live between the fulfilment found in Christ and the consummation which is to come at his return. NT writers using apocalyptic categories would say that Christians live in the overlap of the ages. Christians are described as aliens in a foreign land because they live in 'the present evil age' which will close with the return of Christ. At the same time, they live in 'the age to come' which commenced with Jesus' proclamation of the gospel. The overlap of the ages throws up a dilemma which has troubled scholars.[16] The character of this predicament can be observed if we examine the nature of Christian ethics.

Christian ethics is about applying biblical moral standards to those who have been made new creatures by the work of Christ. Applying the logic of the gospel to the practical lives of the people of faith, Christian ethics is only functional within the community of faith. The reason for this is simple. Christian ethics and the corresponding biblical morality are matters of the heart.[17] Right behaviour and good relationships are dependent on both right thinking and proper motivation. People who by faith are new creatures in Christ are led by the Spirit. They have their minds set on what the Spirit desires (Rom 8:5). Their minds are renewed (Rom 12:1–3). Consequently they are able, in the fellowship of believers and through the study of the Scriptures, to discern what is morally good or in accordance with God's will.[18] Moreover this right behaviour is internally motivated and not externally constrained. Actions spring from a commitment to God and neighbour. The community of faith consists of a group of people who rightly relate to one another in love. It is a community of mutual love relationships.

---

[16] Luther, for example, responded to the dilemma by developing his doctrine of the two kingdoms. However, each of the kingdoms has its own ethic, and the Christian has the problem of operating on two different ethics with two different 'ideals'.

[17] In the Bible the heart generally has to do with that cluster of thinking, feeling, and willing that issues in intentions. Hence hardness of heart has to do with an unwillingness to change one's intentions.

[18] Love is basically a commitment to the good of others. Love and the good are intimately related.

There will be no need of external constraint in the consummated kingdom, for all will have been perfected in Christ. However, this is certainly not the case now. Moral failure is the continuing experience even within the community of faith. The present community of faith is a community where correction initially takes place by exhortation and finally by excommunication (Matt 18:15–20, cf 2 Tim 4:2). Exclusion from the community of faith is the only form of external constraint prescribed in the NT. Dereliction of duty within the Christian community can be repaired through the instruments of repentance, restitution, and forgiveness.

But in the outside world where Christians mix with non-Christians they may encounter situations where there is hardness of heart and no possibility of repair. Ethically speaking two different types of moral advice can be offered on the one issue depending on the context. In 1 Corinthians 7:10,11 Paul commands Christian wives not to separate from their husbands. If they do separate they are not to remarry and the husband is not to divorce the wife. The only alternative to separation is reconciliation.[19] Later, in verses 12 to 16, Paul tells Christians with non-Christian spouses to live together as long as the non-Christian partner is willing. If the non-Christian spouse is not willing to stay, then the Christian is not bound.

Precedence for having two different standards is found in the Law of Moses (Deut 24:1–5). Jesus informs us that Moses allowed divorce in Israel because of hardness of heart. Faced with hardness of heart, Moses is forced to regulate divorce by law in order to restrict the possible harm. Right relationships can only be established where there is mutual love and goodwill. Both Moses and Paul operate on the principle that, where mutual goodwill is missing, action must be taken to prevent harm and secure as much good as possible.

The implication of this way of thinking is clear. In a mixed community where not all are committed to the lordship of Christ

---

[19] The theology behind these commands is that if Christians are committed to working on the Christian model of serving one another in love it is hard to see why they would want to separate or divorce. Some particular difficulties might require separation, but even many of these might be overcome with the diligent attention motivated by true love.

the goal of Christian ethics is not achievable. The goal of Christian ethics is a community of mutual love relationships where each one loves and serves God and their neighbours. Where there is failure of commitment, plus hardness of heart, a context might not allow the operation of the ideal.[20] But love will still operate. In the face of sin love will move to prevent harm and retrieve whatever good it can. Failure to recognise that Christians live in a mixed community as they await the consummation has meant that many Christians have struggled to apply the ideal of the Christian community in contexts where it cannot apply.

The distinction between Christian ethics and retrieval ethics does not imply that there are two moral standards. Rather it is merely the recognition of the fact that Christian moral ideals are applied to two different contexts. In the context of a mixed community the ideal cannot be worked out in full, because some people have no intention to obey God and serve their neighbour. While the final judgment on the actions of these people will come on the last day, governments have the responsibility of restraining these people with a view to keeping good order in the community (see Rom 13:1–7). In this sense the punishment inflicted on people by governments, if it is just, may be said to be the punishment of God.

The shape of Christian ethics

Since Christian ethics is properly a function of systematic theology, any conclusions about the final shape of a biblical theory of ethics based on a brief examination of the nature and shape of biblical theology would be premature.

However, some comment can be made about the way forward. The shape of biblical theology is teleological. The Bible story begins with an order in creation governed by the purposes of God. The story goes on to tell of the fracturing of that order and the neglect of the purposes of God. Wonderfully it tells of the one obedient man who upholds and fulfils the design of the

---

[20] It was this type of context which led Luther to develop his doctrine of the two kingdoms.

Father. Knowledge of God's purposes is restored and the means of recovery established. Kinds and purposes find their true relationships in Jesus. The substance of morality is found in the value of kinds and the true nature of kinds is only detected in their goal or telos. Once God has called creation into being and established his intentions or purposes the content of morality is fixed.

The goal of creation is the kingdom of God. This suggests that an ethical theory based on the Bible might also be teleological. Something like Stephen Layman's theory commends itself.[21] He suggests that an act is right if, and only if, it promotes the kingdom of God. The nature of the kingdom of God is spelt out in terms of harmonious relationships. The kingdom is a place where harmonious relationships are established between God and humans, between individual humans, between groups of humans, between humans and the creation order, and inner harmony within each human.

Conclusion

The task of developing an ethic consistent with the movement and shape of biblical theology is beyond the scope of this paper. In attempting to outline the type of constraints that biblical theology might place on ethics, it has been argued that, while the content of morality has not and cannot change, the understanding of morality can. Christian ethics finds its fullest exposition in the person and work of Christ. The Lord God called on Israel to be holy because he was holy when his people came out of Egypt.[22] The apostle Peter can reiterate this call to Christians in his day (1 Pet 1:16). Christians are to be holy not because God brought them out of Egypt[23] but because they have been given 'new birth into a living hope through the resurrection of Jesus Christ from the dead' (1 Pet 1:3). While the content of morality may be fixed by the orders of creation and the purposes of God

---

[21] C. Stephen Layman, *The Shape of the Good* (Notre Dame: University of Notre Dame Press, 1991).

[22] Lev 11:45b, '. . . therefore be holy, because I am holy'.

[23] Lev 11: 45a, 'I am the Lord who brought you up out of Egypt to be your God . . .'

the understanding of morality (ethics) and its content changes and progresses as the purposes of God are revealed through salvation history. The ultimate and complete understanding of the moral domain is only discovered in the final revelation found in the person and work of Jesus. Morality may not change, but ethics does. The holiness of God does not change, but biblical theology indicates that human understanding of that holiness has and should.

Exploring further

1. What role do biblical and systematic theology play in the formation of Christian ethics?
2. Why is the progressive nature of revelation crucial to understanding (a) sacrifice, (b) law and (c) marriage?
3. How will an ethic based on 'creation ordinances' and an ethic based on the gospel of Jesus differ?
4. How do you respond to the suggestion that an act is right if, and only if, it promotes the kingdom of God?

The Pastor as Biblical Theologian
Graeme Goldsworthy

Synopsis

Biblical theology is integral to a soundly biblical pastoral practice. First, it is important for its power to promote a high view of the Bible. It does this by exposing the inner structure of biblical revelation so that the unity of the message can be seen within the diversity of themes. It shows up the inner consistency of the message, which is a powerful antidote to negative and destructive critical theory. Secondly, it promotes a high Christology by showing us the intricate OT background to the New Testament's teaching about Jesus. Biblical theology guards against superficial and sentimental views of Jesus, so that the call to trust Christ may be made with authenticity. Thirdly, it promotes a high view of the gospel, by helping us to avoid the prevalent errors of subjectivising and internalising the gospel. By preserving the salvation-history perspective of the gospel, the objective 'for us' nature of the person and work of Christ is anchored in history as a finished, perfect, once-for-all event. Fourthly, biblical theology promotes a high view of the ministerial task. A high view of Jesus and his gospel goes hand-in-hand with a high view of ministry.

Biblical theology will banish erroneous ideas of a balanced Christianity in favour of the constant endeavour to find and maintain a biblical perspective on theological truths. It will also challenge the pragmatism that so easily characterises pastoral ministry. Finally, biblical theology promotes a high view of the people of God. The pastor is beset by many pressures which undermine the biblical perspective on the congregation as

Christ's flock. Biblical theology will encourage us to perceive the reality of the church and of the ministries of every member. It should encourage us to take practical steps to implement ministry strategies aimed at the nurture of the whole body of believers and the development of mature ministry patterns.

Introduction

Just as faith without works is dead, so also theological theory without practice is dead. When all is said and done, what should concern the biblical theologian is the effect biblical theology has on faith and works. Since faith comes by hearing and hearing by the word of Christ (Rom 10:17), it is to be expected that there will be some correlation between a grasp of the Scriptures and a passion for God, for his gospel, and for evangelical ministry. The Bible itself warns us that there is a zeal which is not according to knowledge (Rom 10:2). In the situation that Paul addressed it was a Jewish zeal which was not enlightened by the gospel. Those involved in Christian ministry might be excused for supposing that they are immune from the Jewish error, since they understand full well that the one rejected by Judaism is indeed the Messiah.

I was recently invited to conduct a series of Bible studies at one of the home Bible study groups of our church. The chosen subject for study was the book of Proverbs and an inductive study manual had been chosen by the group. When I looked at this book, part of one of the many series of such inductive studies which are presently available, I was astonished at how lacking in any Christian content it was. Being inductive in method, the text was basically a series of questions posed about themes in the designated portions of the text of Proverbs. Even the leader's notes contained little which would help the group relate Proverbs to its context in the wider range of biblical literature. Apart from a few parallels drawn, there was little that would suggest that Proverbs related to the gospel, or that being a Christian actually makes a difference to the way we read this book, or any other.[1]

---

[1] I have attempted to address the matter of the Old Testament wisdom literature in relation to the gospel in my biblical theological study, *Gospel and Wisdom:*

A former colleague once described to me how, while on an overseas trip, he had been taken by his host family to hear a renowned evangelical preacher. He related his embarrassment after the service, because his hosts had enthused about the sermon and obviously expected him to do the same. They were less than impressed when he finally commented that he did not think that the sermon, an exposition from the OT, was a Christian sermon. This may seem to be unduly negative, but it has to be said that much that is preached and written by Christians about the OT differs little from what could well be preached or written by the local rabbi. If there is no explicit gospel content, the only thing left is moralism and legalism.

Elsewhere in this volume I have considered, not uncritically, the work of Geerhardus Vos.[2] Vos was nothing if he was not passionate about his subject. In his 1894 inaugural lecture at Princeton Seminary he discusses the nature of biblical theology and then goes on to say:

> I have not forgotten, however, that you have called me to teach this science for the eminently practical purpose of training young men for the ministry of the Gospel.[3]

He also enumerates some of the expected benefits from a training in biblical theology.[4] First, biblical theology gives to the student a sense of the exquisite structure of the Bible, of its great diversity which is yet brought together by the Spirit of God into one unified truth. Secondly, biblical theology is 'a most effective antidote to the destructive critical views now prevailing'. Thirdly, biblical theology gives new life and freshness to the old truths by showing up the true historical meaning of the texts. And, fourthly, biblical theology is of great value in the study of

---

[1] (continued) *Israel's Wisdom Literature in the Christian Life* (Exeter: Paternoster, 1984). *In The Tree of Life: Reading Proverbs Today* (Sydney: Anglican Information Office, 1993), I have provided a non-technical commentary on Proverbs in the context of biblical theology.

[2] 'Is Biblical Theology Viable?'

[3] G. Vos, 'The Idea of Biblical Theology as a Science and as a Theological Discipline', in Richard B. Gaffin, Jr. (ed), *Redemptive History and Biblical Interpretation: The Shorter Writings of Geerhardus Vos* (Phillipsburg: Presbyterian and Reformed Publishing Co., 1980).

[4] Vos, 21–23.

systematic theology. On the latter point, Vos no doubt spoke out of the context of the evangelical and reformed faith, which placed great importance on the systematic theological task. He saw dogmatics as 'the crown which grows out of all the work that Biblical Theology can accomplish'.[5] These matters are as relevant today as they were a century ago when Vos uttered them. The constant concern for biblical theology in our ministry will have salutary effects on our view of the Bible, of the gospel, of the ministry, and of the people we minister to.

Elsewhere I have discussed some of the pastoral applications of biblical theology, but more needs to be done to encourage Christian ministers to be constantly thinking about biblical theology and its applications.[6] The centrality of the gospel for theology is a focus that all too easily is blurred or simply is allowed to fade away. In my article mentioned above I was concerned to show that biblical theology can be applied in a comprehensive way in the pastoral context, and that it is probably the single most important way of maintaining a gospel-centred perspective in ministry. The practical issues involve, to begin with, helping parents to teach a biblical-theological perspective to their children from the earliest age. Then there is the matter of a Christian education program in the local church which needs to cater for all ages. Preaching, worship, and pastoral leadership can only be enriched by the careful application of the perspectives of biblical theology.

Biblical theology promotes a high view of the Bible

When we speak of a high view of the Bible, people usually think of a high doctrine, perhaps in terms of the supreme authority of the inspired and infallible Scriptures. Certainly, the supreme authority of the Bible over tradition and reason would be a generally accepted mark of evangelicalism. Yet, not only do some evangelicals question the usefulness of such descriptives

---

[5] Vos, 24.

[6] 'The Pastoral Application of Biblical Theology', in David Peterson and John Pryor (eds), *In The Fullness of Time: Biblical Studies in Honour of Archbishop Donald Robinson* (Homebush West: Lancer, 1992), 301–317.

as inerrant and infallible, but the evangelical theory held by some writers does not fit the practice.[7] A form of ecclesiastical popularism and pragmatism easily takes over in our local churches. What works is good. What people respond to with enthusiasm is *ipso facto* biblical. If we are 'stacking them in', then we must be doing it right. The fallacy of such an approach ought to be self-evident but, unfortunately, it is not. People will queue up to purchase the tapes of a series of sermons on a pop-psychology theme, such as self-esteem, while largely ignoring a series of steady exposition of a biblical book. Studies and sermons on Nehemiah the leader, or on Elijah the man who walked close to God, will excite people's sense of the relevance of the OT without ever touching on the theological issue of what God is achieving in the big picture through these people, nor on how such characters testify to Christ. I would not disallow the character study, but its popularity seems to lie in the fact that it draws a line from the biblical character directly to ourselves. It seems relevant, and yet, if relevance has bypassed the gospel, there is surely something lacking in it.

Now, it is true, the expository sermon can easily degenerate into a boring verse-by-verse description of what Paul said to the Galatians or the Corinthians, with no contemporary application. We as Christians believe that not only did Paul speak to local churches but that, through his words, God is speaking to us today. The preacher must be true to the text while at the same time conveying the sense that this is what God is saying to us today. But I, as a preacher, have been as guilty as any in thinking that if someone finds a sermon of mine 'helpful' then it must

---

[7] I do not want to attempt to criticise particular works of evangelicals or to be too specific. I realise that such generalisations could be dismissed as the erecting of straw men. In defence, I can only say that this is my experience. Nor am I implying that the evangelical world is full of disaffection and disloyalty. There are some genuine calls to reassess the traditional evangelical approach to biblical authority, and these must be heard and evaluated. But there is also, I fear, a lack of vigilance with regard to the implications of the gospel for understanding the Bible, which leads to the virtual separation of the grace of God in conversion from the Christian's responsibility to obedient living. It is because the gospel is seen to be what gets us started but not what keeps us going that Christians write and preach about the OT, and about the Christian life in the NT, as if the gospel had no bearing on the matter.

have been biblical. It has to be said that 'helpful' is a singularly unhelpful description, unless we define what it means to be helped.

It would seem that so often we have either all Bible with too little application or all application with little or no Bible. This applies not only to the content of sermons and Bible studies but to the way we do church. All the evangelical cliches about the supreme authority of the Bible count for nothing if our services have become entertainment, if the great doctrinal hymns have been replaced by subjective ditties sung over and over again to some impossible jerking melodies with no recognisable metre.[8] I do not want to digress onto the subject of music here. I only make the point that a stated doctrine of the Bible easily becomes submerged under pragmatism. In our Anglican system the desire for reform and contemporisation can too easily lead us to jettison the biblical structures of our liturgy and practice. And, for the record, I have been to some non-Anglican evangelical services where the Bible was hardly prominent and some where it was not opened at all.

What, then, do I mean by a high view of the Bible, and how does biblical theology promote and sustain it? By a high view of the Bible I mean that once the chosen doctrinal terminology concerning the nature and authority of the Bible has been duly considered and installed, this will be employed self-consciously and with intent as the touchstone for all faith and practice. This may seem to be a matter of spiritual discipline and, to a large degree, it is. But biblical theology can play a significant role in maintaining this discipline in a number of ways.

To begin with, biblical theology exposes the inner structure of biblical revelation as a whole. One of the most exciting aspects of doing biblical theology is the way the interconnectedness of biblical texts keeps surfacing.[9] The more we understand the structure

---

[8] If this seems to be a prejudicial statement, I would hasten to add that there are many objectively excellent contemporary hymns and songs, and many modern melodies that the average congregation can cope with. Nor would I want to suggest that an organ is the only acceptable instrument to accompany congregational singing.
[9] To give one example: during the controversy over the views of the Bishop of Durham regarding the resurrection of Jesus, the bishop was quoted as saying

of revelation within its historical framework, without forgetting the variety of its literary expressions, the more we will understand the relevance of any given text to us as Christians. Quite simply, if we can see how any text relates to Jesus Christ, then, since we also study to know how we as the people of God relate to him, we can grow in understanding of how any text relates to us. Biblical theology helps us to see the unity of the Bible within the complexity and diversity of texts. Having something of the big picture enables us to avoid the wrong application of texts.

When Vos refers to the place of biblical theology as an antidote to destructive critical views, most evangelical ministers would probably identify with him. Not only is a doctrine of Scripture involved, and a whole set of presuppositions, but also a perspective on the unity of the Bible. Vos suggests that we place over against critical theories the organic history of revelation, as the Bible itself constructs it.[10] So much critical theory loses its force when we see the coherence of the Bible as it is taken at face value. Vos makes another important point in this regard when he says, 'The student of Biblical Theology has the satisfaction of knowing that his treatment of Biblical matters is not prescribed for him exclusively by the tactics of his enemies'.[11] This is an important point, because much evangelical comment on biblical criticism is merely reactionary. As important as such an apologetic is, we need to assert our own presuppositions and follow them up to the point where we can show the self-consistency of them and the power of their coherence in explaining reality, which includes the reality of the Bible. Biblical theology helps us to show the self-consistency of evangelical presuppositions, because it shows up the internal consistency of the biblical story.

---

[9] (continued) we did not need knock-down miracles to impress us. The idea that the resurrection was no more than a miracle story calculated to impress totally misses the point which a biblical theology of the resurrection emphasises. Biblical theology helps us to see the connection between all the promises of God to Israel, and Jesus the true man of God and faithful Israel. Even in the thinking of some evangelicals, it would seem, the resurrection of Jesus is mainly the final stage of revelation about life after death. It is that, but it is much more.
[10] Vos, 22.
[11] Vos, 22.

Biblical theology promotes a high view of Jesus

From one point of view this subject could be dealt with under the next heading concerning the gospel. However, it is important to make a distinction between Christology and the soteriology of the gospel even though, in the final analysis, Jesus is the gospel. A great deal hangs on what we understand about Jesus of Nazareth. If we want to discourage people from the kind of popular piety that borders on sentiment rather than faith in the Son of God, we need to be well acquainted with the testimony of Scripture to the person of Jesus. The study of biblical theology is important here, for it not only assembles the titles and attributes of Jesus assigned to him in the NT, but also burrows away, as it were, into the foundations of these themes in the OT.

When Hans Küng wrote his monumental book *On Being a Christian*, he asked a disturbing question: 'Which Christ?'[12] If we are to proclaim Christ, which Christ will we proclaim? Is it, asks Küng, the Christ of popular piety, the Christ of dogma, the Christ of the enthusiasts, or the Christ of literature? To ask the question is not to presuppose the answer but only to flag the danger of being seduced from a truly biblical view of the Christ. Broadly speaking, I suppose there are two main ways of pursuing the subject of Christology. The one is a biblical theological approach,[13] and the other is the philosophical and dogmatic approach.[14] Both are necessary, but the need for a thoroughgoing biblical theology approach is not always appreciated at the level of pastoral ministry. We need to have some idea of the irreducible minimum that needs to be stated about Jesus when we are inviting people to put their trust in him. Have we not all at some time heard the evangelistic sermon that calls on people to come to Jesus without having given the slightest idea as to why and on what basis?

Such a biblical theological approach to Christology is characteristic of the four gospels. Whether it be the birth narratives

---

[12] Hans Küng, *On Being a Christian* (Glasgow: Collins, 1974), 126.

[13] An example of this more descriptive approach would be Oscar Cullmann's *The Christology of the New Testament* (London: SCM Press, 1959).

[14] For example, Dietrich Bonhoeffer, *Christology* (London: Collins, 1966).

of Matthew and Luke, the creating Word prologue of John, or
the prophetic fulfilment theme in Mark, the gospels all begin
by drawing biblical theological threads together in their por-
trayal of Jesus. This Christ is very different from one presented
in so many distortions and cliches of word and song. When
biblical theology shows us how all the great themes about God,
his people, and the promises are gathered together in Christ,
then faith in Christ takes on a meaning that is all too rarely
attained.

Biblical theology promotes a high view of the gospel

Biblical theology engenders a high view of the gospel. History
illustrates this point, for the loss of the objective gospel in the
early church appears to have gone hand-in-hand with the loss
of the historical and natural meaning of the OT. The allegorical
spiritualising of the OT in the medieval church gained greater
acceptance than did the Antiochene typology. The former down-
graded the historical meaning, so that a notion of salvation-
history was largely obscured. Biblical theology languished
under the regime of allegory. Typology, by contrast, saw the
historical acts of God in the OT as the preparation for and the
structure of the gospel event.[15] Thus, it was no coincidence that
Luther's re-establishing of the objective historical gospel event
accompanied his recovery of the historic meaning of the OT. As
we wrestle with what we might call the historico-theological
links between the testaments, we are forced to reckon with the
gospel as objective historical event. This has a daily impact on
evangelical ministry.

If ever there was an emphasis that needed recovering in
evangelical ministry today it is that of Luther's 'alien' righteousness. Many evangelicals think and preach more like Bult-
mannians (the gospel is what happens in the pulpit on Sunday
morning) or Thomists (the gospel is what happens when the
grace of God flows into my soul), while the major subjective

---

[15] See my books *Gospel and Kingdom* and *According to Plan* for further treatment
of allegory and typology.

thrust of Charismatic thinking is decidedly pre-Reformation (the Spirit's work in my life becomes the gospel). It is all a matter of perspective. To assert the objective nature of the gospel is not to deny the subjective or existential truths of Christian experience. It is important to maintain that the gospel is what really happened in history in the person of Jesus of Nazareth, while the grace of God in me, the encounter with God in the preached word, and the work of the Spirit in my life, are all the fruit of the gospel which depend for their effect on the objective gospel. A biblical theological view of salvation-history helps us to see that the distance between us and the gospel event is not merely one of days and years, but is also one of theological distinction between what God did for us then and what God does in us now. Salvation-history helps us to maintain the real distinction between the finished and perfect gospel event and the unfinished and not yet perfected fruit of the gospel in our lives.

When the loss of salvation-history led to the blurring of the gospel, Rome fudged by redefining the grace of God as a spiritual influence appropriated primarily through the sacraments and changing the Christian's life until justification is achieved. Evangelical and charismatic pietism differs from this Romish view mainly in rejecting the mediating role of the sacraments and the church. However, the notion of grace as Jesus living his life in me is substantially the same as the Catholic view rejected by the Reformers. The important biblical doctrine of the new birth has been highjacked from its biblical theological context and elevated to become the essential gospel. Jesus-in-my-heart theology, which is so prevalent in evangelicalism, is a reversion to Catholicism, in that the essential gospel is not what took place for me back there in salvation-history but what takes place in us now. In practice much evangelical ministry concentrates more on what God can do in our lives now, at the expense of what God has done for us in the life, death, and resurrection of Jesus. Of course both are valid aspects of the biblical teaching, but it is the perspective that becomes distorted. Biblical theology and a sense of salvation-history is of immense value in maintaining the biblical perspective on the relationship of God's work for us and God's work in us.

Biblical theology promotes a high view of the ministerial task

It might reasonably be asked how a concern for biblical theology should affect the way I conduct my ministry. Would it not be better to remain reserved about this matter and to suggest that the gains will be intangible and very general? Or might we not be bold and claim that biblical theology will have real and observable effects in our lives and ministries? I prefer to think the latter, provided, of course, that we exercise our responsibility to work at it. The first point is that, if biblical theology promotes and maintains a high view of the gospel, it will also promote a high view of gospel ministry. There can be no more potent antidote to pragmatism than the constant reinforcing of the truth that the gospel is the power of God for salvation.

Once again, biblical theology will help us to maintain a right perspective on what constitutes the gospel that is the power of God. It will also preserve us from downgrading the significance of the word *salvation*. When we see how biblical theology unfolds salvation as the whole process by which God brings us and the whole of creation to the appointed consummation, we are less likely to be sidetracked by pop-psychology and similar fads. One hesitates to criticise such things lest it be taken to indicate that we propose a purely theoretical and 'cerebral' approach to Christianity. The problem is that popular opinion does not usually tolerate the finer, if important, distinctions. People generally are impatient with distinctions; it is seen as hairsplitting. Thus, if one suggests that something which is good has usurped the place of something better, or the best, one is likely to be accused of rejecting this good thing altogether. Like the word 'helpful', the word 'balance' is unhelpful here. It is not a question of balancing biblical truths, since they seldom do balance. Try balancing divine sovereignty with human responsibility. There is no balance at all! A better word is 'perspective', for there is always a biblical perspective that we must strive to uncover, even if we have, at the end, to declare that it is a mystery. The concept of balance has led to some of the more inane cliches which are in fact quite inimical to the gospel perspective. Balance leads to anaemic theology and compromising practice. It

presupposes that the relationship between two things is simply
a matter of giving equal time to each. It avoids the question of
the nature of the real relationship between things. It is often a
failed attempt to remove the mystery from God and his ways.
Stay with *perspective*![16]

One of Vos's points was that biblical theology was important
for the study of systematic theology. This is not the place to
explore the relationship between the two, but I would suggest
that they are mutually supporting. A minister who is thinking
in the framework of biblical theology will want to contemporise
that process and bring out the relevance of biblical teaching to
people today. Systematic theology involves this process of making contemporary what is in the Bible. Possibly one of the
reasons why some ministers cease to think theologically is that
they do not connect that activity with their daily Bible reading
and sermon preparation. When exegesis does not lead to biblical
theology, and when biblical theology is not pursued into systematic theology, then the exegetical task easily remains isolated at
the level of unreflective proof-texting. Thus, part of the process
of bringing out the relevance to us of given texts is to show that
behind the specifics lie the theological principles stemming from
who God is and what he is like. We need the big picture if we
are to think theologically and to grasp what really is going on in
our lives and in the world.

Any parish minister understands that there is a constant
struggle to establish priorities for time and tasks. Ministers are
increasingly expected to be efficient and effective chief executive
officers of fairly complex local church organisations. Once again
pragmatism easily takes over. Without underestimating the
problems, it has to be said that the office of pastor-teacher is first
and foremost the office of theologian. The role of biblical theology in this relates to the fact that it interacts with the necessary
abstractions of systematic theology and ties them to the history
of redemption and of the people of God. In practical terms,
biblical theology resonates with the reading and expository

----

[16] *Balance* is a perfectly good English word, and it is not without its uses, even
in theology. What I am objecting to is its being used merely to signify that two
things are true and belong to our concern.

preaching from the Bible week by week, and with people's reading of the Bible at home. People who protest that they are simple Bible believers and have no time for theology need to be ministered to. Biblical theology can be a bridge to the formulation of at least a rudimentary systematic theology. And systematic theology, in turn, becomes the formal basis for understanding oneself before God and in the world. When Christians see that there is a biblical doctrine of doctrine, and that it stems from the recognition that we are heirs to the whole wonderful process of salvation-history culminating in Jesus Christ, then perhaps they will show a little more enthusiasm for doctrine. The minister who has become the overworked CEO-manager of a large and diverse organisation is likely to have little energy or time to attend to such a pastoral matter.

Biblical theology promotes a high view of the people of God

During a course in biblical theology that I teach at Moore College, one of the overseas students came to me and expressed appreciation for my emphasis on the believer's union with Christ. It was not, he said, an emphasis that he had heard much of at home. It was an emphasis that grew out of the biblical theological survey of the people of God from Adam to Abraham, from Israel to the remnant and the Servant, and finally to the last Adam, the seed of Abraham, the true covenant Son of God, the faithful Israel and the Servant, namely Jesus Christ. This is a biblical theology which culminates in the resurrection of Jesus and the exaltation of his humanity to the presence of the Father. By faith every believer is united to Christ in his death and resurrection. This is a fact which not only has eternal consequences, but which defines each Christian and the identity of the congregation of believers.

It is the eternal consequences of the gospel which give it the central place in evangelical thinking and practice. As Bernard Ramm puts it:

> Because the evangelical still maintains the real distinction
> of saved or lost and not merely Christian or non-Christian,

he cannot shop theologies or review theological options like the person who holds no such conviction_At this point the evangelical is least understood, for his salvation is linked to his theology which is not the case with non-evangelical theologies.[17]

It is this dimension of eternity linked to the biblical gospel which charges the evangelical view of the people of God. Yet, it is easy to actually downgrade the people of God into the core membership of an organisation. They are perceived in practice as financial supporters of the institution and the voluntary helpers in a multitude of activities, some good, some indifferent, some positively inimical to the gospel. Let the pastor and people study the great themes of the people of God through the method of biblical theology. Let them ponder the wonder of it all that the process that began with Adam and Eve and which is consummated in the visions of the book of Revelation of the people of God worshipping before the throne of God and the Lamb, is really and truly the process into which our local church is caught up.

A biblical theology of the people of God at worship is a biblical theology that will boost the eradication of the notion of pew-warming. Of course not everyone will catch the vision, but if pastors and their eldership do not grasp it, no-one else is likely to. If there is any validity to the growing conviction among evangelical congregations that every Christian is given the role of a servant, a minister, then it is time for this theology of every-member ministry to start to shape the way we organise our parish life and our ministerial activity. Despite some excesses, particularly emanating from charismatic sources, concerning the subject of spiritual gifts, we can be thankful that the idea is gaining ground that every church member has ministry to perform. People don't just go to church, they are now understanding that they are the church.[18] Once we recognise the nature of the people of God as

---

[17] Bernard Ramm, *The Evangelical Heritage* (Waco: Word, 1973), 149.

[18] It would be churlish not to recognise the positive contribution made by many charismatic churches and writers to the recovery of this important perspective. However, it also needs to be said that there were some notable evangelical voices lifted in this cause long before the charismatic or neo-pentecosta l movement took off in the early 1960s.

ministers we will also recognise the place of Christian education. Christian education has largely been seen in terms of Sunday school and the confirmation class leading to a passing out ceremony. We know that is not what it is meant to be, and we have striven in various sporadic ways to address the need for adult Christian education. The small-group movement has had quite an effect but, due partly to its origins, has sometimes involved a less than biblical philosophy of Christian nurture.

A fairly typical parish scene would be something like this: the main Sunday morning service includes the children for the first part and then, at a convenient point, the children leave and go to Sunday school. The adult church continues and includes a sermon. When this is concluded with maybe a cup of coffee, everyone goes home and that's it for Sunday. During the week the keener ones gather in small groups, some weekly, some less frequently, and engage in various kinds of programs ranging from Bible study to caring and sharing and even 'house church'. There may be some more planned programs offered such as 'Christianity Explained' or some of the Moore College external studies courses. You may, of course, feel that a church that works as well as that is blessed indeed! I want to suggest that even when things are this good, the connection is rarely made between being saved to serve as a minister in God's people and a planned program of training and biblical education. I turn now to consider some of the practicalities of such a program.

Some practical issues

Biblical theology in the local church ministry must begin in the pastor's study. If it doesn't start here it may, by the grace of God, start with some theologically informed laity, but it will not have the impact that comes from leadership in the matter. In speaking of biblical theology in the pastor's study I don't mean simply that pastors should set aside a regular time slot for reading biblical theology as part of their wider program of theological reading. There is only a limited amount of biblical theology available to the Christian public. But I would encourage the minister to see biblical theology as a way of thinking that needs to be cultivated about all issues of pastoral ministry. It is a method of approach to almost any matter that confronts us in ministry. It is a way of training ourselves in theological reflection that will pay handsome dividends if we persevere.

Let us consider some practical examples of the kind that confront the pastor in the course of pastoring, and the Christian in the course of living as a Christian. Sometimes there are no clear dogmatic formulations and we are left with a few Bible verses that spring to mind, along with a certain amount of experience-based wisdom. It is in such cases that biblical theology comes into its own. Whether the subject is prayer, knowing the will of God (guidance), assurance, the fulfilment of prophecy, secular powers, miracles, Israel and the Palestinians, social justice, suffering, the sabbath, leadership, life after death, church and denominations, or whatever, biblical theology provides a strategy for investigation. It enables us to make progress on subjects that don't turn up in concordances (because they do not involve a single biblical word) nor in handbooks on doctrine (because they are not perceived to be doctrinal matters of importance).[19]

While I was serving as part of a parish team-ministry, it was for a number of years my task to propose on an annual basis the shape and content of the preaching program. In time I developed an approach to give the right priorities to various kinds of sermon. At the top of the list of priorities was the expository preaching from recognisable units of Bible text, rather than on 'texts' consisting of a verse or part of a verse. As a matter of discipline, I included series of sermons from different kinds of biblical literature and made sure that the OT was well represented. Then it was a matter of working in some systematic doctrine.[20] For several years I included an annual series of five or six sermons based on the Thirty-Nine Articles. This was not a lot, but at least it kept the notion of official Anglican doctrine and its biblical underpinning before the congregation. Another

---

[19] In my book *According To Plan* (Leicester: IVP, 1991), chapters 26 and 27, I have suggested a method of approach to such topics using a biblical theological method.

[20] All sermons should be doctrinal, but there should, I believe, also be sermons from time to time which focus on doctrine as such rather than on a given biblical text. Sometimes a sermon can do both, which is a bonus.

series included at least once a year would focus on topical matters and ethical issues such as abortion and homosexuality. Finally there was the inclusion at least each year of a series of eight or nine sermons on some biblical theological theme. We covered topics such as creation and new creation, salvation, covenant, the temple, and the people of God.[21]

The aim of such a sermon series would be, broadly speaking, to teach biblical theology and both content and method. As to the content, it would aim to show the development of the great themes of the Bible in order to uncover their significance in their final expressions in the NT. It would aim to develop a sense of the spiritual or theological unity of the Bible. And, most importantly, its aim would be to proclaim the real Christ of the Bible. As to the method, the aim of a biblical theological series would include that of encouraging people to read the Bible for the big picture rather than being locked into the search for inspiring thoughts from individual verses.

The value of the biblical theology series lay in the way it seemed to help people gain the big picture and to develop a more coherent sense of the message of the Bible. A practical issue in such a series is whether one needs to make some link in each sermon between the early stages of the theme in the OT and Christ, or whether it can be left until we arrive at the NT end of things. There is a difference between the weekly sermon and a series of Bible studies. In the latter, where the same people attend week by week, the gospel fulfilment of the OT themes can perhaps be left to unfold in a biblical theological way, though Christians in discussion will probably raise the issue of fulfilment. But a series of sermons in church involves more of a floating population. We would all like to see the whole congregation there every Sunday. The reality is rather different. If half are there on a weekly basis we are probably blessed. There will be a proportion who attend regularly, where 'regularly' means

---

[21] So, for example, a series on the new creation could start with 2 Cor 5:17, or even Rev 21:5, and then proceed to examine what lies behind these texts: creation; fall; Israel redeemed to be a new people in a new land flowing with milk and honey; Isaiah's vision of the new heavens and earth with the temple and Zion; Jesus as the new temple in his incarnation and resurrection; Rom 8 and the new creation.

perhaps once a month. There are those who come sporadically, and there are those who enter at a venture for whatever reason and without any firm intention to repeat the experience. Such a congregational make-up indicates that every sermon should not only preach Christ and him crucified, but that it should be clearly perceived so to do. This presents us with a challenge, for in a sense it means that we have to be creative enough to make the links with the gospel in a legitimate way and also in a way that does not lead the more regular hearers to say, 'Ho hum; here comes the Jesus bit'.

Biblical theology, as it leads us to a greater awareness of the gospel and the people of God, should also be the core in a program of Christian education. I have expanded on this in my article in the Donald Robinson *Festschrift*.[22] I will reiterate some of the main points. First, in the home biblical theology is an important dimension in the nurture of Christian children. This means that the parents will need to understand the structures of biblical theology. And it also means that we desperately need writers of children's literature who can incorporate a biblical theological perspective into their works.

Sunday school curricula need to come under close scrutiny to see if the perspective is biblical. Again there is a great need for writers of such material who understand biblical theology and who have a philosophy of Christian nurture which is gospel-centred and not given to moralising. It is understandable that study material for teenagers will often be problem- or issue-centred. But using such an approach to create interest should not take over and govern the whole pedagogic intent. Biblical theology should be commended to Christian teenagers as a way in which they can learn to think and behave biblically when dealing with the contemporary issues facing them. A totally inductive approach to issues that concern teenagers can easily lead to the pooling of ignorance. A totally deductive approach is likely to instruct with a few chosen proof-texts and pat answers. Such a prescriptive approach usually falls into legalism and moralising. Biblical theology provides the framework from within which Christian young

---

[22] See footnote 6.

people can learn to think and act responsibly, and to apply principles to the issues of life.

When it comes to adult Christian education it seems to me absolutely basic that we should work towards the time when everyone who aspires to a teaching ministry or a leadership position undertakes a course in biblical theology. Those in high school, no matter how keen, should not be given leadership and teaching roles in Sunday school, even at the kindergarten level (some would say especially at that level) until they have done the requisite training. Also, one sermon a week is definitely not enough training for the leaders of home groups. There needs to be flexibility in such groups, and they need to minister to different kinds of people with different kinds of needs. But they should not be the opportunity for the sharing of unbiblical ideas. If this sounds rather imperial let me say that to resort to pastoral dictatorship would be a denial of all that I have been trying to convey in this article. Let us recognise the difference between encouraging lay leadership and teaching roles, and a policy of *laissezfaire* in which any unqualified person who aspires to it can exercise what he or she considers to be a teaching ministry.

I conclude with these few observations. My own experience in pastoral ministry led me to realise that we do not live in a perfect world, and we certainly do not minister in perfect churches. Much of what I have said may seem to be out of reach simply because any change from what exists is just too hard; the upheavals would be too great. Ministers coming to a new parish have to reckon with the tension between what exists and what they, after a reasonable period of due consideration, think ought to exist. People resist change, and it is not in the scope of this paper to consider strategies for change. But quite radical changes can be achieved. They may take time, but they can take place. With a minimum of upset the minister can set up training classes for teachers and small-group leaders. Biblical theology should be the core item on the agenda. Begin to include sermon series (start with shorter ones) on biblical theological themes. Make sure there is some good biblical theology on your church bookstall, and educate the person who runs the stall to promote good theological literature. Finally, I would make this rather daring assertion in which I am being absolutely serious. When Paul said to the Ephesian elders (Acts 20:27) that he did not shrink from declaring to them the whole counsel of God, he was, of course, referring to biblical theology.

A Suggested Bibliography of Biblical Theology for Pastors[23]

Books

Bright, J., *The Kingdom of God.* New York: Abingdon, 1955.

Clowney, E.P., *Preaching and Biblical Theology.* Grand Rapids: Eerdmans, 1961.

——, *The Unfolding Mystery: Discovering Christ in the Old Testament.* Leicester: IVP, 1988.

Dumbrell, W.J., *Covenant and Creation.* Exeter: Paternoster, 1984.

——, *The End of the Beginning: Revelation 21–22 and the Old Testament.* Homebush West: Lancer, 1985.

——, *The Search for Order: Biblical Eschatology in Focus.* Grand Rapids: Baker, 1994.

Goldsworthy, G.L., *According to Plan: The Unfolding Revelation of God in the Bible.* Leicester: IVP, 1991.

——, *Gospel and Kingdom: A Christian Interpretation of the Old Testament.* Carlisle: Paternoster, 1981.

——, *Gospel and Wisdom: Israel's Wisdom Literature in the Christian Life.* Carlisle: Paternoster, 1987.

——, *The Gospel in Revelation.* Carlisle: Paternoster, 1984.

McComisky, T.E., *The Covenants of Promise: A Theology of the Old Testament Covenants.* Nottingham: IVP, 1985.

Peterson, D.G., *Engaging With God: A Biblical Theology of Worship.* Leicester: Apollos, 1992.

Strom, M., *Days Are Coming: Exploring Biblical Patterns.* Sydney: Hodder and Stoughton, 1989.

VanGemeren, W., *The Progress of Redemption.* Grand Rapids: Zondervan, 1988.

---

[23] This list does not include any of the many Theologies of the Old or New Testaments. Nor is there any attempt to provide an exhaustive list. It is a suggested list of books and articles that, to varying degrees, should be helpful to pastors in keeping a feeling for biblical theology alive in the midst of busy and demanding ministries. Some of those still in print could be considered for the church bookstall.

Journal and *Festschrift* articles

Carson, D.A., 'Current Issues in Biblical Theology'. *Bulletin for Biblical Research* 5 (1995), 17–41.

Goldsworthy, G.L., 'The Pastoral Application of Biblical Theology', in David Peterson and John Pryor (eds), *in the Fullness of Time: Biblical Studies in Honour of Archbishop Donald Robinson* (Homebush West: Lancer, 1992).

——, 'The Great Indicative: An Aspect of a Biblical Theology of Mission', *Reformed Theological Review*, 55/1, 1996, 2–13.

Scobie, C.C., 'The Challenge of Biblical Theology', *Tyndale Bulletin*, 42/1, 1991, 31–61.

——, 'The Structure of Biblical Theology', *Tyndale Bulletin*, 42/1, 1991, 161–194.

——, 'New Directions in Biblical Theology', *Themelios*, 17/2, 1992, 4–8.

Exploring further

1. Suggest a series of six sermons on the biblical theological topic of the promised land. What other topics lend themselves to this approach?
2. How could you ensure that your youth and Sunday school leaders understand the overall unity of the biblical message?
3. To what degree is it necessary to give a summary of the OT background to Christology every time you preach an evangelistic sermon?
4. What are some practical ways people in your congregation could be encouraged to a better understanding of biblical theology?